Rusty Bresser and Sharon Fargason

BECOMING SCIENTISTS

Inquiry-Based Teaching in Diverse Classrooms, Grades 3–5

Stenhouse Publishers
Portland, Maine

Stenhouse Publishers
www.stenhouse.com

Library of Congress Cataloging-in-Publication Data
Bresser, Rusty.
    Becoming scientists : inquiry-based teaching in diverse classrooms, grades 3–5 / Rusty Bresser and Sharon Fargason.
        pages cm
        Includes bibliographical references and index.
        ISBN 978-1-57110-978-1 (pbk. : alk. paper)—ISBN 978-1-57110-995-8 (ebook) 1. Science—Study and teaching (Elementary) 2. Inquiry-based learning. 3. Multicultural education. I. Fargason, Sharon, 1949– II. Title.
    LB1585.B67 2013
        372.35'044—dc23
                                                                                    2013011208

Cover design, interior design, and typesetting by Martha Drury

Manufactured in the United States of America

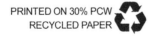
PRINTED ON 30% PCW
RECYCLED PAPER

19 18 17 16 15 14 13   9 8 7 6 5 4 3 2 1

*Rusty would like to dedicate this book to Sandra Arkin,
who introduced him to inquiry science.*

*Sharon would like to dedicate this book to her students—
past and present—whose excitement about science and
inquiry has helped her become a better teacher.*

CONTENTS

Becoming Scientists: Inquiry-Based Teaching in Diverse Classrooms *uses real stories of active, student-centered learning to show the reader inquiry science in action. An easy-to-read conversational tone weaves educational research with practical, best practice strategies demonstrated as classroom examples. The experiences of an exemplary elementary teacher define a clear target for all educators, novice and veteran, to design learning environments and experiences that support inquiry learning for all learners.*

—Sharon Bowers, Secondary Science Presidential Award Winner; Educator in Residence, Center for Integrative STEM Education at the National Institute of Aerospace

This book holds the key to training the next generation of engineers. The style of inquiry-based instruction advocated by Bresser and Fargason encourages students to be autonomous thinkers and doers, equipping them with the skills and confidence necessary to tackle the types of open-ended and ambiguous problems that are ubiquitous in engineering practice.

—Brandon Reynante, Mechanical and Aerospace Engineer, ATA Engineering; Elementary Science Educator

An important work! A timely work! A must-read for educators dedicated to providing authentic science experiences for today's youth. Drawing upon both research and actual classroom practice, Bresser and Fargason provide a guidebook of sorts for practitioners to navigate their way into and through the Next Generation Science Standards, enabling teachers to see a model of how to facilitate learning experiences that will allow diverse learners from all backgrounds to engage in the "doing of science," while grounding their learning in the core ideas and crosscutting concepts outlined in our newest educational standards. So many books out there tell you *about best practices; this one truly* shows you how to *enact best practices. This is the way for students to learn science—to grapple with real issues and think critically to solve problems we face today and in the near future. Bresser and Fargason have provided the science educational community with a clear vision of how inquiry science can be taught so that all students can fully participate and begin to close the achievement gap in science.*

—Rachel Millstone, Codirector, California Science Project, University of California, San Diego

FOREWORD

The Next Generation Science Standards (NGSS) is intended to support a vision for a science classroom where students of diverse backgrounds and English language abilities are all actively engaged in the practices of science, and where core ideas and crosscutting concepts emerge from those practices. Such a classroom is one where the teacher and students are engaged in authentic scientific inquiry. What might such a classroom actually look like, and how can teachers prepare themselves for enacting this new vision of inquiry science? This very readable book, coauthored by Rusty Bresser and Sharon Fargason, provides substantive answers to those questions. Focusing both on the research base and on real classroom examples, the authors lay out a plan to help teachers, administrators, and science educators transform the NGSS vision into practice.

Let me share a story from Sharon's classroom to illustrate why I'm excited about *Becoming Scientists*. A few years ago, Sharon joined a professional development project that I was involved with that encouraged teachers to try a new approach to their science teaching. Rather than designing lessons aimed at guiding their students to achieve specific content objectives (for example, district-mandated benchmarks), we wanted teachers to design their classroom activity around their students' own ideas. We wanted teachers to listen carefully to the substance of students' ideas and reasoning, and to make their next-move decisions based on the merits of those ideas. We referred to this strategy as *responsive teaching*. Thus, the sequence of what would happen in the science classroom each day would not be predetermined, but instead would occur in response to the students as they proposed, critiqued, discussed, and tested their ideas.

The teacher might have certain core ideas in mind that he or she wanted students to learn, but with responsive teaching those ideas could emerge from the students' engagement in scientific inquiry. Sharon seemed quite intrigued with this idea of responsive teaching; it just seemed *natural* to her. She knew this could be a challenge, especially since her classroom was very diverse and most of her students would be English language learners. Nevertheless, she decided to try it out at the beginning of the following school year.

While other teachers at her grade level were using the district-mandated curriculum module about the earth, moon, and sun for the first third of the school year, Sharon spent the first half of that time teaching responsively, using the context of toy cars as a way to teach about the earth, moon, and sun. (The project staff had suggested that toy cars might be a good context for generating a lot of student ideas.) She thought things were working well and decided to have her students think about phenomena related to the earth, moon, and sun, but instead of following the mandated curriculum, she continued teaching responsively, following the students' own ideas. She never even had the students open the book provided for the curriculum. When it came time for the district's benchmark test on the earth, moon, and sun unit, she decided to have her students take it, even though her principal had agreed (as part of Sharon's participation in the project) that they did not have to do it.

As it turned out, Sharon's class did spectacularly well on the district's benchmark test. The percentage of her students who performed at the proficient or advanced level was significantly higher than the average in the school district. I asked Sharon why she thought her students did so well. She told me that during the test itself, two things happened that she had not experienced before. First, she noticed that several students seemed to be actively involved with their bodies as they were answering questions, as if they were imagining the relative positions of the sun, earth, and moon. Second, when she was reading some of the questions to her English language learners and then recording their multiple-choice answers on the test sheet, several of the students spontaneously tried to explain their reasoning to her, even though that was not elicited. It seemed that Sharon's students saw test taking as a making-sense activity rather than as an information-recall activity. These students were used to thinking, and they were evaluating the various answer options to try to figure out which made the most sense.

I think this story illustrates the power of responsive teaching in helping all students see themselves as active sense makers as they explore and think about the natural world. When students are in such a classroom, they are engaged in legitimate scientific inquiry. They come to expect that their ideas matter—that the questions they raise, the experiments they propose, the conclusions they draw, and the scientific arguments they engage in are all valued. All the students in Sharon's classroom were engaged, regardless of their cultural background or ability to speak, read, and write English. Sharon was so pleased with how things were going in her responsive teaching classroom that she decided to continue using that approach during all her subsequent science teaching. Over the years that followed, Sharon developed a great deal of wisdom and insight into how to teach science responsively in a diverse classroom, and she shares that wisdom and those insights in this book. It should be no surprise that many of Sharon's strategies that seem to promote success in her science classroom are supported by research in teaching and learning.

In this book, Rusty and Sharon have made a strong case for using an inquiry approach with students who have been historically underserved by our educational system. They structure many of the chapters around first raising and problematizing important issues involving teaching and learning inquiry science, especially in diverse classrooms, often drawing on the research base for support. Then they provide specific strategies to address the issues and illustrate each strategy with rich examples from Sharon's classroom experiences.

This book is important to the science teaching and education community and to school administrators, because it provides a practical way of addressing the true spirit of the Next Generation Science Standards in elementary classrooms, especially ones with diverse student populations. The many interesting examples throughout the book from Sharon's own classroom show the power of student thinking and engagement. As the authors say in Chapter 5, "Most important to being a good science teacher is holding the expectation that *all* children can be scientists and think critically." Starting with this stance, and focusing on engaging all students in real scientific inquiry as described in this book, a teacher can not only help students achieve the NGSS, but also help prepare them for success as future learners.

Fred Goldberg
Professor of Physics,
Center for Research in Mathematics and Science Education
San Diego State University

ACKNOWLEDGMENTS

We would like to thank the following people. Without them, this book would not have been possible:

Toby Gordon, for her editorial expertise and guidance.

Jay Kilburn, Chris Downey, Rebecca Eaton, and everyone at Stenhouse who shepherded our book through the production process.

The students at Fay Elementary, who continue to inspire us!

Fred Goldberg at San Diego State University and David Hammer at Tufts University, whose ideas about science have inspired much of our writing.

Lynn Susholtz, for the time she put into taking and editing photographs.

Cesar Bohorquez, for making the journey complete.

Becky McRae and Melanie Speros, for taking the leap into inquiry, and for allowing us to document and share their wonderful teaching.

Eileen Moreno, principal at Fay, thank you for your enthusiasm and support.

Tina Rasori, for opening her classroom to us.

Kathy Melanese, for her editorial feedback on Chapter 4.

Marilyn Burns, who is a constant inspiration and model for teaching for understanding.

The authors would also like to acknowledge each other for a wonderful year of friendship, collaboration, and learning.

CHAPTER 1

INTRODUCTION: WHAT IS INQUIRY?

I remember the first time that I was excited about learning science. It was 1963, and one of my fellow third graders had brought a land tortoise to school. Everyone gathered around the giant, prehistoric-looking reptile and gazed in amazement at the ancient creature. Ten pairs of little hands rubbed the smooth yet bumpy shell and spontaneously began asking questions. I wonder how old he is. Why does he have such a big shell? Do you think he can live to a hundred years old? How fast can he walk in an hour? Which foods do you think he likes best? Can he swim in water like the turtle I have at home? The questions kept coming, and they weren't from the teacher. In fact, the teacher was nowhere in sight. Some of our questions were research questions that could be answered only by reading books, talking to a tortoise expert, or going on the Internet (if there had been an Internet back then). Other questions were testable ones that could have been explored firsthand through experimentation.

Although I wasn't aware at the time that we were engaged in the beginning stage of inquiry science—by starting with our own questions about the world—I did feel the excitement, motivation, and curiosity that seemed alive and palpable all around me. Inquiry science has little to do with textbooks and lectures and everything to do with our inherent need as a species to learn about and reflect on the world around us. Humans, and particularly children, are natural scientists, and it seems that nothing can stop us from inquiring about our world, except for maybe the classroom.

I remember the buzz of excitement about our new reptile friend came to an abrupt halt with the scolding voice of our teacher, summoning us to the classroom where we began the "real" science lesson. Textbooks were opened, voices quieted, and the teacher in all her wisdom began her lesson about desert animals: she lectured and we passively pretended to listen. I'm sure most of us were still thinking about the tortoise and imagining all the neat experiments we could do with it.

"Learning science is something students do, not something that is done to them" (National Committee on Science Education Standards, National Research Council 1996, 20). This quote from the National Science Education Standards sums up nicely what inquiry science is all about: active, student-centered learning. When we engage in inquiry, we begin with a question. It could be a question that comes from children who are responding to some stimuli or topic. Or, it could be a provocative question posed by the teacher at the beginning of a science unit. We then move to designing experiments that test our question. During experimentation, we collect data, make discoveries, and draw conclusions about our question. Finally, we come to new questions that fuel the next cycle of inquiry. In inquiry science, children learn about concepts by being involved in the science processes. They observe and describe objects and events, make predictions, ask questions, acquire knowledge, construct explanations of natural phenomena, test those explanations in many different ways, and communicate their ideas to others. They do exactly what grown scientists do.

Doing science in the real world outside the classroom is a messy business, and is open to interpretation and change. While testing their hypotheses, scientists work together, make mistakes, start over, ask new questions, and try to control variables that pop up unexpectedly. They work from prior knowledge and experience and follow their hunches into the unknown. There is no neat and tidy textbook plan for them to follow. Theories are built, torn down, and replaced over and over. If you don't believe me, ask Aristotle! His theories about physics were replaced by

Newton's theories, and then most recently by Einstein's. Scientists learn about the world the same way that children do: by their active participation in problem solving and critical thinking.

Although we know that scientists in the workplace are immersed in the inquiry process, work collaboratively, and share their discoveries with others, teachers in some classrooms still rely heavily on textbooks, lectures, and rote memorization when teaching science. Oftentimes, science is not taught at all, because "more important" subjects such as reading and math must be taught since "they're on the test." Although traditional approaches to science instruction are still in play, there has been tremendous progress in science teaching. In California, for instance, hands-on science kits from FOSS: Full Option Science System (Lawrence Hall of Science 2012) have worked their way into classrooms. These kits come with teacher guides and lessons that are aligned to state standards, include hands-on experiences, offer performance-based assessments, and provide opportunities for students to participate, in various ways, in the 5-E Instruction Model: Engage, Explain, Explore, Elaborate, and Evaluate (Carr, Sexton, and Lagunoff 2007). Although the kits are fairly structured in their approach, the lessons allow students to become actively involved in learning science.

While hands-on science is finding its way into classrooms across the country, researchers in science teaching and learning are discovering that an inquiry approach can have a positive effect on student achievement, especially for poor students and for those learning English as a second language. For example, researchers in the southeastern United States studied the effects of inquiry learning on groups of students from culturally, linguistically, and socioeconomically diverse backgrounds in six different schools and found marked improvement in test scores (Cuevas et al. 2005). Other researchers of science education have compared inquiry-based instruction with "commonplace" or traditional teaching, and the results support the effectiveness of an inquiry approach (Wilson et al. 2010). And although inquiry can enhance learning, it has also been found to be the most effective way of increasing appreciation for science (Ornstein 2006).

HOW CHILDREN LEARN SCIENCE: THE ROLE OF NAÏVE CONCEPTIONS

An abundance of research tells us that children construct their own knowledge by testing ideas and approaches based on their prior knowledge and experience, applying these to new situations, and integrating the new knowledge with preexisting intellectual constructs. These preexisting ideas can serve as fertile ground from which new understandings grow. Watson and Konicek (1990), in an article describing a fourth-grade teacher's efforts to "teach for conceptual change," paraphrase Louis Pasteur's conclusion that "understanding favors the prepared mind." They go on to echo Eleanor Duckworth, pointing out that children need to develop a network of ideas in which to embed new ideas. For example, if Sonia, a third grader, already believes that sunlight and plant growth are related because she's thought about and experimented with plants over time, she's likely to assimilate the idea that depriving plants of light may be detrimental to their health (Abruscato 2004). But sometimes the ideas that children bring to new learning experiences are flawed and based on erroneous assumptions or partial information. Responding to children's naïve conceptions about the world and offering experiences that help them confront their previously held conceptions is at the heart of an inquiry approach.

Children derive their naïve conceptions through limited observation and experience (Yin, Tomita, and Shavelson 2008). For example, children may have partial or surface-level understandings of where energy comes from, based on their observation that "things work if they are plugged into the socket in the wall." From these initial conceptions about energy, children move toward more complete understandings of how energy is stored and transferred through social interaction and direct experience, not necessarily by being told or shown by the teacher. Furthermore, children may generalize that "flat things float" because they've observed rafts and surfboards during outings at the beach. Unless they see, through further experimentation, that flat pieces of iron or ceramic plates sink, they may hold on to their previously held beliefs about buoyancy. Without investigation, children may continue to think that when an object is at rest, no forces are acting upon it; that the shape of the moon always appears the same; that mealworms are worms; that sweaters create their own heat; that seeds come from a packet; that rocks must be heavy; or that you grow on your birthday. In fact, children hold on to their notions with a passion. Teaching by telling does not necessarily help students change their conceptions. We cannot drag children into understanding concepts that have taken scientists sometimes years to make sense of just because the test is looming or because the pacing guide says we have to be on page 38 by Friday. The beauty of inquiry science is that it is based on asking good questions, providing rich experiences that confront naïve conceptions, and allowing students to learn about the world like scientists. Inquiry science supports the notion that good teaching is more about listening to children and asking key questions than telling and showing.

Inquiry science is not something new. For a long time, teachers on the cutting edge of science instruction have been teaching children to think, reason, and problem solve. Guided by research about how children learn, these teachers have pushed ahead despite pressures from certain stakeholders who would prefer to see them teach to the test. Sharon Fargason is one of these educators. In the following paragraphs, Sharon describes her own journey as a learner of science, shares her view of the teacher's role when teaching inquiry science, and articulates how the approach described in this book is different from traditional and hands-on methods.

WHAT HAPPENED TO THE BANANA I THREW IN THE COMPOST PILE?

A few years ago I was invited to join a group of teachers at a summer institute. We would learn some science, talk about pedagogy, and reflect on our lessons throughout the year. That sounded good to me. A little learning, a little more spending money. Sign me up! A few weeks before the training started, I received an e-mail asking me to start a compost bin at my house. I had no idea what that meant, but a quick Google search gave me a plethora of options for compost bins. They ranged from tiny ones that sat on your kitchen counter to massive installations for your backyard. Being the urban girl that I am, I bought the tiniest one I could find, put it on my back porch in an effort to keep the flies away, and dumped some fruit peels into it every now and then.

I went to the summer institute wondering what they were going to teach me about compost bins. I was excited because the topic was "green" and earth conscious, and I wondered if I could bring my own personal experiences to the institute. I came with my notebook already prepared: a section each for procedures, observations, findings, and vocabulary. I was a good student, and I was ready.

"How many of you started a compost bin?" asked the presenter.

I raised my hand, yawned a little, sipped some coffee, and settled into my chair, ready to hear what she had to say about my bin.

"So I put a bunch of stuff into mine," she said, "and it doesn't look the same anymore. What happened to the banana peel that I put into my compost bin?"

I wrote the question down and waited . . . and waited . . . and waited. No one said anything. We sat waiting for some direction, a project, a lecture, readings, something. When the silence became too uncomfortable, a brave soul squeaked out a response. "It rotted."

"What do you mean?" asked the presenter.

"I don't know," said the brave soul after several silent seconds. "It just rotted. It's gone."

"Hmmm," said the presenter. "I wonder what that means. Where did it go?"

What do you mean where did it go? I wondered. *That's what you're supposed to tell me!* I sipped some more coffee and sank into my chair. *This is going to be a long week*, I thought. I heard a lot of silence before someone brought up bacteria.

"What is bacteria?" asked the presenter. "And what does it do to my banana peel?" Something in her question made me think of my tooth, which I had recently had filled at the dentist. So I threw in my contribution.

"Well, I know that bacteria ate my tooth and put a hole in it, so I had to have it filled," I said.

I wasn't sure if it had anything to do with what we were discussing, but it broke the silence, and for me, that was good. But my comment made sense to someone, and she expanded on it. Pretty soon we had a pretty good conversation going about bacteria! Not my usual favorite while drinking my morning coffee, but it intrigued me and got my brain spinning. Before I knew it, I was in front of the class drawing a diagram of bacteria and how it "ate" the banana peel and pooped it out, creating a new substance that was a kind of fertilizer that helped other plants grow. I didn't know if it was correct (still don't), but it made sense to me and seemed to explain some phenomenon I had experienced in my life. It also didn't answer our questions completely.

We had plenty more. How come my compost bin smelled horrible and others' didn't smell at all? Was it really bacteria eating the fruit peels or some other microorganism? Was the mush left in the compost bin chemically different from what was put in? How come some stuff accidentally left on your counter becomes rock hard and other stuff becomes a gooey, rotten mess? How come some wood left out in nature becomes petrified and some rots? Why didn't one person's untreated wood deck rot?

We spent the morning asking questions, debating, talking about our own compost piles, drawing pictures, thinking, and thinking some more. It was riveting, and I was hooked. My brain was exploding with ideas, and

I was having a lot of fun thinking about the plausibility of all the ideas I had heard. I was making connections to things I had seen, and that seemed to be sufficient for all the professional scientists who were our presenters. At one point, someone even told me that I was really good at science. Me! It always took me ages to understand anything scientific, and I was certainly not used to hearing stuff like this. But the compliment was not about my scientific knowledge or memory. It was about the way I was thinking about things and the connections my mind was making. I went home a happy camper that day. I felt like a scientist. I felt smart, and I couldn't wait to go back the next day.

Many of the ideas in this book are based on Responsive Teaching in Science, the project I participated in that was funded by the National Science Foundation. (For more information about the project, see the Responsive Teaching in Science website: http://cipstrends.sdsu.edu/modules/index.html.)

During my time on this project, I learned and practiced the art of inquiry science. My experience with the compost bin and the way that I came up with so many ideas without being told what was correct ignited a fire in me that I set out to light in my students as well.

INQUIRY SCIENCE AND HANDS-ON SCIENCE: WHAT'S THE DIFFERENCE?

I recently sat on a committee in my district whose task was to choose the new science curriculum materials that our district would adopt. As I sat through presentation after presentation by many different publishers, I realized that most curriculum materials have recently added some kind of hands-on approach. Some models focused mainly on getting information from readings and included projects or experiments, which reinforced these texts. Other curriculum models started with experiments and progressed into readings and videos, and they all came with a myriad of ways to differentiate the reading for struggling students or English language learners—book passages on CD-ROM, leveled book passages, and songs that reinforced the content. The resources in these curricula were wonderful and very comprehensive.

A unit in a typical hands-on or guided-inquiry science curriculum includes directions for how to introduce a topic, some projects or experiments for the kids to do, some readings or videos to supplement the learning, and worksheets for the students to practice their learning and show their understanding. There is a prescribed order in which things are taught, and there are pacing guides to follow and instruction manuals to read. Although this approach to teaching science has elements of inquiry in that it can allow children to ask and pursue their own questions, it is usually highly structured and is generally more teacher-centered than child-centered.

Our approach to science is different and might be characterized as open inquiry. In open inquiry, there is a general plan, but there is no particular set of instructions for how a unit should go. Instead, the students' thinking, discoveries, and questions guide the teaching. Usually, the teacher starts with a question and the students take it from there. They share ideas, ask each other questions, try things out, and ask more questions; they engage in the inquiry cycle. The students inquire and the students determine where the learning goes. Although they may decide that they want to look something up in a book or consult the Internet, there are no prescribed readings or recipes of scientific explanations. There are things the kids need to learn. As teachers, we are required to cover the standards, but in inquiry science we help students uncover and discover the content of the standards rather than reporting them and asking the students to memorize them.

Thus, the role of the teacher becomes very different from the way it looks in a typical hands-on curriculum. The teacher inspires inquiry by posing provocative questions, facilitates conversations, makes experimenting possible, and encourages in-depth thinking. Although the role of the teacher is important, the students take the front seat. They have a hand in guiding the curriculum, and this curriculum might change each year.

Inquiry science is not, however, a free-for-all. The students are the drivers, but not every direction they want to go in is wonderful. It is the job of the teacher to listen for ideas that are clear and have merit, because they either explain a certain phenomenon or describe an experience that will help other students make sense. Their ideas do not have to be correct. In inquiry science the students try to determine what is correct by thinking about what actually makes sense and by trying things out, much in the same way professional scientists (who do not have books to turn to since they are discovering new things) work toward finding correct information.

Although the students take the front seat in guiding what happens in a lesson, the teachers have responsibilities that go beyond posing questions, encouraging great thinking, and making experimentation possible.

They must also provide extra support for students so that they are able to engage in conversations that help make inquiry possible, especially if the children come from diverse backgrounds, are not economically advantaged, learn in different ways, and might be learning English as a second or third language.

TEACHING AND LEARNING INQUIRY SCIENCE IN DIVERSE CLASSROOMS

Although the inquiry approach that Sharon has described requires students to construct their own understanding of how the world works through experimentation, reflection, and discussion, not all children are given the opportunity to engage in these activities. Many children, especially those who are underserved and underrepresented at universities and colleges, are often provided with a very different kind of science education.

In *Poor Teaching for Poor Children?*, Alfie Kohn writes about the "pedagogy of poverty" and how "children in low-income neighborhoods are most often exposed to a curriculum that consists of a series of separate skills, with more worksheets than real books, more rote practice than exploration of ideas, more memorization than thinking" (2011, 32–33). In his article, Kohn describes a talk by British educator David Gribble, who speaks in favor of the kind of education that honors children's interests and helps them think deeply about questions that matter. Of course, Gribble added, that sort of education is appropriate for affluent children. For disadvantaged children, on the other hand, it is . . . essential. Inquiry science is indeed essential for all students, especially because while the student population in the United States is increasingly racially, ethnically, and linguistically diverse, science achievement gaps have persisted by race, socioeconomic status, and language (Next Generation Science Standards Writing Team 2012). This book, in part, is a response to the National Research Council and the Next Generation Science Standards call for equity in science education. "Equity, as an expression of social justice, is manifested in calls to remedy the injustices visited on entire groups of American society that in the past have been underserved by their schools and have therefore suffered severely limited prospects of high-prestige careers in science and engineering" (National Research Council 2012, 278). In responding to this call, our book addresses important issues faced by teachers who teach science to diverse student populations.

How do you teach inquiry science when your students come from many different linguistic, cultural, and socioeconomic backgrounds? How do you support your students when your class is made up of a wide range of learning styles, skills, and support from home? How do you build upon students' varied experiences, background knowledge, and readiness? How do you meet the needs of students with varying levels of English language proficiency?

SUPPORTING ENGLISH LANGUAGE LEARNERS

Driving through the neighborhood that Sharon's school serves, you get the feeling that you are traveling somewhere in the developing world, but it's hard to identify exactly which country you are in; the cultural diversity is striking. Mexican taco shops, Chinese fast food, East African thrift stores, and Vietnamese pho restaurants line the main boulevard. The families that send their children to Sharon's school belong to many different ethnic groups; thousands are refugees from Africa and Southeast Asia, 70 percent of the people in the community are the working poor from Latin America, and 40 percent are living below the federal poverty line. The children at Sharon's school make up what is a truly diverse community of learners who have roots in Mexico, Guatemala, China, Thailand, Burma, Somalia, Vietnam, Ethiopia, and Cambodia. Some are African American, and a few are European American. They speak thirty-four different native languages, and 80 percent are English language learners who need extra support in all academic areas, especially in science. Since we use language to learn by sharing our own ideas and hearing the ideas of others, inquiry can provide an ideal context for using language to learn science and using science as a context for developing both social and academic language in English. Research has shown that "discovery or inquiry-based science instruction is an effective means for helping ELL students successfully learn science concepts and develop English language skills" (Wright 2010, 251).

Learning science through inquiry can potentially benefit language learners, but it can also put these students at risk, especially if the language of instruction (English in this case) is foreign to students. English language learners face a triple challenge: learning the social aspects of a second (or third) language, the academic language specific to the content area (in this case, science terms and discourse), and the academic content. English language learners can become lost during whole-class discussions or during partner talks unless the teacher plans for structured support to help them access the content and say something about their learning. Like their native English-speaking counterparts, these students may be unfamiliar with the academic terms being used during an experiment or investigation, but they may also be unfamiliar with the language structures in English that are necessary for them to describe, compare, predict, or hypothesize.

Sharon's school is a perfect place to witness how an inquiry approach to teaching and learning science can benefit all students, but especially those who are often marginalized, are underrepresented at universities, and do not typically perform as well on standardized tests as their native English-speaking, middle-class counterparts at other schools. This book is structured in such a way as to provide the reader with a clear vision of how inquiry science can be taught so that all students can fully participate and begin to close the achievement gap in science.

THE BOOK'S CONTENTS

This book is intended for a wide audience, including classroom teachers, administrators, preservice teacher candidates, and professional development leaders. Our intent is to paint a picture of what an approach to inquiry looks like in grades three, four, and five, and how providing the right support can allow all students to experience success in science.

In Chapters 2 and 3, Sharon describes ideas and strategies that can help teachers think about how to plan, teach, assess, and manage the classroom when teaching inquiry science to diverse student populations. These guiding principles are brought to life through examples that all teachers can relate to and thus employ in their own teaching.

Chapter 4 offers specific strategies for helping all students, particularly English language learners, access science content and communicate their science learning in English.

Chapters 5 and 6 take the reader into actual classrooms to see how the strategies and guiding principles highlighted in Chapters 2, 3, and 4 are implemented.

In Chapter 7, Sharon uses examples from the classroom as she responds to teachers' frequently asked questions about teaching inquiry science in diverse classrooms.

And in Chapter 8, Sharon models, through inquiry, different ways that teachers can deepen their understanding of the science concepts and standards that they are responsible for teaching.

INTEGRATING THE NEXT GENERATION SCIENCE STANDARDS

According to the National Research Council (www.nextgenscience.org/) science practices are the behaviors that scientists engage in as they investigate and build models and theories about the natural world. The Next Generation Science Standards (Next Generation Science Standards Writing Team 2012) call for teachers to integrate into their lessons important practices that help students think and work like scientists, and become successful analytical thinkers who are prepared for college and careers. These practices are especially important for students who have traditionally been underrepresented in science, technology, engineering, and mathematics (STEM). The vignettes in this book provide powerful examples of these science and engineering practices that include the following:

- *Asking* questions
- *Developing* and using models
- *Planning* and carrying out investigations
- *Analyzing* and interpreting data
- *Using* mathematics and computational thinking
- *Constructing* explanations and designing solutions
- *Engaging* in argument from evidence
- *Obtaining*, evaluating, and communicating information

TAKING THE LEAP

We recognize that teaching science in the manner described here has its challenges, especially if you are a teacher who is overwhelmed by the amount of material you are expected to teach, or if you are restricted by a pacing guide that requires you to follow district-adopted materials. We encourage you to use this book as a way to open up what you are already doing. Maybe this means asking more open-ended questions, listening a little more and telling and showing a little less, letting the children come up with an experiment on their own, feeling okay with the confusion that happens when an experiment doesn't turn out the way you expected, supporting language learners in new ways, or modeling inquiry and learning right along with your students. And for those of you who have the freedom and flexibility to take the leap into inquiry science, we say, take that leap! Your students will show you their appreciation through their increased engagement and motivation to learn science.

The lessons and ideas in this book are not intended as blueprints to be followed step-by-step, but rather as guidance and inspiration for teachers as they explore the world of inquiry science with their students and work toward narrowing the achievement gap that has left many language learners and minority students behind.

CHAPTER 2

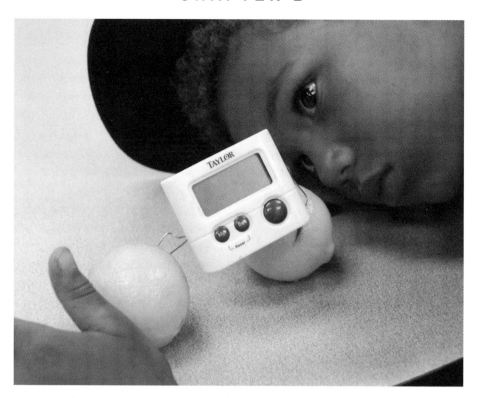

GUIDING PRINCIPLES FOR TEACHING AND LEARNING INQUIRY SCIENCE

Albert Einstein once said, "It is nothing short of a miracle that the modern methods of instruction have not entirely strangled the holy curiosity of inquiry" (Rogers 1972, 301). Although many of the "modern methods" Einstein was referring to were in practice decades ago, teaching science as inquiry still faces great obstacles today. Much progress has been made in science education, especially with the implementation of hands-on science kits that move instruction toward inquiry, but many educators, for a variety of reasons, continue to hold on to traditional practices when teaching science. Teachers are responsible for more now than they have ever been, and they risk criticism and pressure if they don't conform to the status quo. Barriers to teaching from an inquiry approach often come in the form of questions. What will happen if I don't understand all of the

15

science content? What if the students are confused and I don't have the answers to their questions? How do I assess student progress if I teach from an inquiry approach? How much do I tell and how much should I let my students explore and discover? Will I get in trouble if I deviate from the science curriculum guide? What will happen if I give up control and let the kids talk, work in groups, move about, and handle science equipment? What if I don't know how to respond to children's science ideas, especially when they are incorrect? How do I teach inquiry to children from a variety of backgrounds, often different from my own?

In this chapter, Sharon uses examples from her own experience, episodes from her classroom, information from research, and metaphor as she offers ten guiding principles that are intended to allay teachers' fears, offer advice, and instill a sense of excitement for teaching inquiry science. Most important, these guiding principles will help educators design effective science learning environments for all students.

TEN GUIDING PRINCIPLES

Following are ten principles that I use to guide my teaching. These ideas are fundamental for creating a successful inquiry-based classroom.

1. You Don't Have to Know Everything

During my first experience with inquiry science, I spent a week trying to understand the decay process that happened inside a compost bin. Once I got into the process, I started working on drawing and explaining a diagram that modeled what I thought was happening to the chemical composition of the fruit peels in the compost heap. Midway through my explanation, one of the lead scientists on the project came over to listen to my thoughts. I tentatively offered my ideas and then said, "I don't know. Is that right?"

I'll never forget his answer: "I'm a physicist, not a biologist. I'm figuring this out with you. Let's keep thinking about your explanation and see if it makes sense to us." I was shocked. Here was a brilliant scientist with a résumé that would put anyone to shame, working alongside me, pondering whether my ideas could be scientifically sound. Even he didn't have all the answers. But he had an excitement for inquiry and the confidence to pursue the investigation with me. He inspired me to want to find the answers for myself, and he provided me with the support that I needed.

A study commissioned by WestEd and conducted by the Lawrence Hall of Science at the University of California-Berkeley in 2010 found that, although almost 90 percent of teachers felt very prepared to teach English language arts and mathematics, only about one-third felt very prepared to teach science (Dorf et al. 2011). In fact, less than 2 percent of elementary teachers hold a bachelor's degree in a scientific field. Understandably, teachers often don't feel prepared to teach scientific content, since they don't think they have adequate knowledge themselves. That's the bad news. The good news is that it is possible to do your own learning and investigations so that you can teach inquiry science well. When students are engaged in inquiry science, they are questioning, hypothesizing, testing, explaining, measuring, comparing, and so on. They aren't depending on or memorizing facts given in a lecture from an expert.

In *Best Practice: New Standards for Teaching and Learning in America's Schools*, Steven Zemelman, Harvey Daniels, and Arthur Hyde write the following:

> *When we consider the teacher's role in the science classroom we must recognize that lecturing is not only unsupportive of hands-on investigation, but also that research shows it is strikingly unsuccessful at influencing students' science concepts. The teacher needs to model the same kinds of questioning and problem solving that he or she wishes the class to learn. Fortunately, this means a teacher need not have all the answers or be an expert in all areas of science.* (2005, 120)

Modeling scientific behaviors, it turns out, is much more important than knowing all the answers.

In my class's investigation of energy, there were many times when a student asked a question and I was left stumped. What happens if we turn the batteries upside down? Will the flashlight still work? What if we attached rechargeable batteries to a solar panel and left them out in the sun? Would they recharge? How do you store the energy that is created from a windmill? These were wonderful questions, and I had no semblance of an answer for any of them. However, instead of sweating over the thought of showing my students that I didn't know everything, I used the opportunities to model the behaviors I wanted them to learn. I showed curiosity in my responses. "That is a really interesting question! I don't know the answer to that, but I would love to investigate. What could we do to try to find out?" I listened intently to the students' answers, and I made sure to ask questions when I didn't understand or wanted to know more. I wrote notes and was purposeful about checking out books from our class trip to the library that might be helpful. I offered my own ideas and showed my delight when students questioned them. We didn't always find solid answers to our questions, and sometimes when we read something, we agreed that we didn't really understand the "answer" and would have to investigate more. My students gained some powerful knowledge that went beyond the set curriculum. They learned that science is about having questions and investigating them. Next time when they wonder about something, I hope they won't feel as though they need to wait for an expert to tell them the answer. My hope is that they will dig right in like professional scientists do and start investigating!

2. Kids Know a Lot More Than We Think They Know

Our students come to school with a vast amount of scientific knowledge. They have spent their whole lives as little scientists—observing, comparing, wondering, and testing. Consider a four-year-old gazing out the car window, wondering why the moon is following him wherever he goes, or a kindergarten student who asks how the vegetables his parents always made him eat helped him grow so tall that he needed to buy new pants. These children are already involved in inquiry science.

I was recently chatting with a friend at her house while her nine-month-old baby methodically played with the carpet square on which she was lying. She rubbed her hand over the top and then turned the corner over and felt the underside. She did this over and over until her three-year-old sister asked why she was destroying her neat little play area. Her mom explained that the baby wanted to know how each side of the carpet felt. She was exploring, and she was successfully thinking like a scientist with no help at all.

Unfortunately, in school, there is so much content to be covered that we often spend less time encouraging kids to continue being scientists and more time filling them up with information. The first time I taught my students about the water cycle, I knew that there were many academic vocabulary words and difficult concepts they would need to understand, so I broke my unit into pieces and taught the kids one word and concept at a time. I started with evaporation. I taught them the word; we developed a hand motion to go with it, sang some songs about it, and did a project where the kids could watch evaporation happen in a jar. Condensation came next, and we followed the same procedure. We breezed through precipitation because I knew that my kids had a lot of experience with rain—

they simply needed to know the scientific word to go with it. I taught my students what they needed to know about the water cycle, but I didn't honor the science they had already done on this topic. They needed me, the teacher, to give them a forum to explore further and the tools to take their thinking beyond their initial findings. As Zemelman, Daniels, and Hyde write, "[G]ood science teaching involves facilitation, collaborative group work, and a limited, judicious use of information giving" (2005, 75). Students need time to work on their questions and refine their ideas. They don't need the answers handed to them.

Our students have seen puddles form on the ground during a rainstorm and found that they disappeared the next day when the sun came out. They have seen steam rising over the spaghetti pot and have felt their water glass get wet as it sits on the table. They need help putting these concepts together and realizing that they have some questions about what's taking place. The next time I taught my class about the water cycle, I pointed out a dry spot on the playground where there had been a huge puddle we had all had to jump over the day before.

"Where did the puddle go?" I asked. Hands shot up and kids were excited to answer.

"It evaporated!" one answered.

"Hmmm," I said. "What does that mean—it evaporated?"

"The sun dried it up."

"Interesting idea," I said. "What does that mean? Did it just disappear?"

During our conversation, several kids answered my questions with vocabulary they had heard in previous grades, and when I asked what they meant by those particular words, we realized we had a lot of questions:

> If water evaporates, condenses, and then precipitates, how come it
>   rarely rains in San Diego even though we have the ocean right
>   next to us?
> Does salt evaporate along with the water in the ocean?
> Will spilled milk evaporate?
> Where does mist come from?
> Why is the grass on the field always wet in the morning?

We worked on these questions together. The kids used what they already knew, and sometimes they tried an experiment they thought might answer one of their questions. Sometimes when we were talking about our observations, I gave the kids the scientific vocabulary word to go with it; they would talk about how water collected on the mirror after they got out of the shower, and I would tell them that scientists would use the word *condensation* to describe water that collected like that. They still learned all the vocabulary and the important concepts, but I held back my lectures and honored the science they already knew and wanted to know more about.

3. Science Is a Team Effort

Even scientists who are noted for working alone often have a team to "play" with. Charles Darwin wrote hundreds of letters to discuss his ideas and get feedback from colleagues before he published them. You see, a scientific idea is just that. It is an idea that needs to be shaped, expanded, and refined. Today we know that the world is round, but many years ago the idea of a flat earth was widely accepted. It was a good idea, based on empirical evidence, but since science is a "team sport," others questioned and disproved this notion, making it possible to go deep-sea fishing without fear of falling into an abyss.

Doing science makes me feel like I am in a good soccer game. I have the ball and am headed down the field, but I am suddenly stuck with nowhere to move without losing the ball. I could take a giant kick and aim for the goal, but I know better than that. Luckily, I spot a teammate over to my left, and I swiftly pass him the ball. He passes it back once he notices that my opponents have moved on, and I kick the ball toward the open player waiting near the goal. She taps the ball past the goalie and into the net, and we've scored a point. We've scored a point—not the last player to touch the ball. That was a team effort, and we are all proud. Had any of us tried to do that on our own, we would have lost the ball in a jiffy.

Students in our classrooms need science to be *more* like a team sport. They have ideas that need to be refined and reshaped. They often have the same ideas as scientists throughout history, but teachers have the benefit of knowing how these theories have changed and been disproven in previous years. When students say things that we know are incorrect, it is tempting to correct them right away or steer them toward the right answer. However, we must realize that our students have a room full of little scientists sitting next to them who would love to be part of the team and contribute. Why not let them work together, kick the ball around a little, and see if they get it in the net before we take over and tell them what to do (see Figure 2.1)?

I remember being extremely uncomfortable the first time I taught my students about the sun, moon, and stars. One student in my class pro-

Figure 2.1
Science is a
team effort.

posed the idea that the earth stays in one place and the sun and the moon switch places so that we have day and night. I wrote the idea down on our chart and bit my tongue when I wanted to explain why that wasn't possible. The idea was widely accepted in my class. A couple of students asked for models of how this would work and seemed fine with those provided. They showed the sun and the moon slowly traveling around the earth, each on opposite sides, so that one side of the earth was in daytime and the other side in the darkness of night. Then one day, a student noticed the moon was out while we were walking to lunch. "Wait a second," he said. "I thought the moon was on the other side of the earth since we are seeing the sun." Soon the other students were talking about this discovery, and our theory (which had been working until now) was disproven. It took some time for them to get there, but I was glad I had bitten my tongue. The discovery was powerful and meaningful to them because it was theirs. It was their teamwork that got them where they needed to be.

As much as I want to be on my students' team, I need to be the coach—setting up the plays and strategizing for the big picture of the game. But I cherish those moments where I can put my coach's hat aside and join them on the field, because I truly don't know all the plays by heart.

4. Models Help You Explain and Understand What Others Are Saying

Remember in elementary science class when you built that model of the solar system? Or maybe you constructed a model volcano and made it erupt with a combination of baking soda and vinegar. I made a cell using hair gel in a plastic bag. That was my favorite. I still remember all those enjoyable activities, but they did little to build my scientific knowledge. I was simply re-creating something that someone had already done. I usually looked in my textbook and found a picture to use as a reference, and then placed my Styrofoam planets or jelly bean mitochondria in the appropriate spots.

Alternatively, models (either oral or physical) can be tools that scientists use to communicate their thinking in a way that is understandable to others. I remember my dad comparing my arm to a neuron when I was having trouble with my freshman physiology class in college. "Your arm is like the axon of the nerve," he said. "Your hand is the cell body, and your fingers are the dendrites trying to connect with another nerve." His model was incredibly simplistic and covered only the basis of what I needed to know, but all of a sudden, I understood neurons and had a way for organizing my information.

In a class discussion about energy, one student was trying to explain his argument that a toy car would travel faster on a long shallow ramp than a shorter, steeper one. He was excited about his idea but wasn't able to communicate his reasoning. Finally, he shared that the longer ramp gave the toy car time to gather up energy like a snowball gathers snow as it travels down a hill. It might be worth noting that the student's idea was, in fact, incorrect. However, his model allowed the other students in the class to enter into a discussion with him that would not have been possible in his original tongue-tied state.

Models can also be a tool used to test out a particular theory or idea. For instance, a student who has seen diagrams of the sun with the moon orbiting the earth may suggest that this is the reason that the moon "changes shape." Instead of simply accepting that this is correct, a teacher may suggest that a model be created to test the idea (see Figure 2.2). It is important to note that models can quickly become "fun activities" if not used carefully. A teacher who hears an idea from a student and suggests creating objects that could be used to try it out is helping the student use models as part of the scientific process. However, when modeling is taught as a way to *explain* a fact, the students may no longer be engaged in scientific modeling.

Figure 2.2
Models can be created to test out students' ideas.

Models can be a wonderful way for students to explain and test things that go beyond what is tangible and easily accessed in a science classroom. When used correctly, models help children engage in scientific behaviors rather than soak in scientific facts.

5. Good Ideas Aren't Always Scientifically Correct

Karen, a fifth-grade student, listened closely to a discussion her class was having. They were trying to figure out why people in Australia don't fall off the earth into space. One student suggested that it's because of gravity, and the teacher asked what gravity is. After a long silence, Karen proposed that gravity is something in the air that pushes you down so that it is impossible to float away. Although her idea isn't quite scientifically correct, Karen's comment stirred a whirlwind of comments and questions.

"I wonder why you float away if you are on the moon."

"I know that if you go skydiving, you have to use a parachute so that you fall to the ground slowly. Gravity is working way up there. If there is something in the air, I wonder how high it is."

"Yeah, and if it's way up there, how come it works when we are down here on the ground? Even if I jump just a little bit, gravity pulls me back down."

Karen's idea wasn't accurate, but it was a good idea. It made sense and explained a phenomenon that she had observed in her life. It was a jumping-off point, a place of entry for other students to add their observations, questions, and theories.

Thomas Edison had about a thousand ideas that were not scientifically accurate before he invented the lightbulb. He failed a thousand times, but each failure led him one step closer to the discovery that you and I depend on each day. Edison made hypotheses, tried them out, and then tweaked them when they didn't work. If everything came out right the first time, science would be obsolete. It isn't *what* you know, but *the process of finding it out.*

Teachers often tell me that there is a big difference between Edison and modern-day students trying to determine why they don't float off into space. We *know* the answer. It's probably even written in the fifth-grade textbook sitting on their desk. Isn't it important that students learn accurate information? Yes! It is definitely important. However, if we never give students the time and the space to grapple with ideas, we are robbing them of skills that might help them make important scientific discoveries in the future. Students need to know that science is something you *do*, rather than a list of facts and formulas that need to be memorized. A student taking a college-level science class is unlikely to remember the facts and information taught in elementary school. However, the attitudes and habits of mind created as students engage in inquiry are more likely to stand the test of time.

6. Disequilibrium Can Trigger Sense Making

Several years ago, I was teaching my first-grade students about how plants grow. The curriculum suggested that we try growing plants in different conditions to see which ones grew. Then we would be able to deduce what conditions were actually needed. We put one plant in the sun and watered it twice a week. We put one in the sun and never watered it. We put one in a dark closet and watered it twice a week, and we put one in a dark closet and never watered it. Then we wrote down our predictions for which plants would grow. Since I was the teacher (which meant I clearly knew the answer), I didn't share my predictions, but I privately guessed that the only one that would grow would be the plant in the sun that we diligently watered. I knew plants needed light and sun to grow, so those in the dark closet had no chance whether they were watered or not. The class was diligent about watering our visible bean sprout sitting on the windowsill, but the poor plant in the closet got watered only once or twice. *Oh well,* I thought. *It wouldn't have grown anyway.*

Two weeks after we started our experiment, I pulled the plants out of the closet so that we could discuss them the next day. The kids had gone home for the day, so I collected the plants in the front of the room and made a label to go in the front of each: "Sun + Water," "Sun + No Water," "Dark + No Water," "Dark + Water." The first plant looked beautiful. The second, not so much, but that is what I expected. I pulled out the bean that had been in the closet and not gotten any water. It was a barren wasteland—also what I expected. I pulled out the last plant and gasped when I saw it. A little white sprout was curling out of the dirt. I was shocked. How in the world did this plant grow with absolutely no light?

I did two things that afternoon. The first I wish I could take back. I yanked that little plant out of the dirt and placed the pot of dirt up on the desk. I didn't know why that grew, and I didn't want to confuse the kids. The second thing I did was to launch my own investigation about seed performance in the dark. I put several lima beans on a wet paper towel and left them in the dark closet. I checked them periodically. They all sprouted, but never seemed to grow more than an inch. I was so confused. I asked every teacher at my school. "Do you know why that happened?" I looked in books and checked the Internet. I learned that seeds need only water to sprout. Then they need light to keep growing after that.

My failed hypothesis put me in a state of disequilibrium that I desperately wanted to sort out. I was amazed by my curiosity, because I couldn't have cared less about plants when the unit started. I had watched plants grow a lot of times and had read a lot of textbooks about the subject. I was just going through the routine so that my students would know the same information I did. I wish I could take that day back. If I could do it again, I would show the class how surprised and curious I was; I would let them help me come up with new experiments to do. My whole class would enter a state of disequilibrium with me, and their potential to learn would increase greatly.

7. A Student's Background Affects His Interactions with Science

I cherish the fact that my students come from so many different backgrounds. As a class, we get to see and hear about the world from many different perspectives. I have some students whose parents love science and talk about it at home. These students come to school confident of their content knowledge and ready to pass it on to everyone else. They often become more pensive down the road when another student challenges or disproves their ideas. On the flip side, I have students who have never heard the word science in their lives, but have seen things firsthand that I have only glimpsed in books: a rain forest, a tsunami, the East African savannah. They may sit back, observe and listen for a while, but when they have gathered their thoughts, they often share something quite profound.

We know that a student's background affects the lens through which he or she views the science classroom. Take weather, for example. A student from New York will have a much different perspective on winter than a student from San Diego. And a student from an equatorial country knows only two seasons: wet and dry.

But background can also affect the way students communicate and interact with materials. Last year I had several students from Thailand who were often quiet during discussions. When I was getting to know their parents in the beginning of the year, one mom explained to me that many Thai children are taught to respect the teacher. She said that in her village, children were told to sit quietly and that they should never speak to an adult unless the adult asked them a question first. This mom was thrilled that I was encouraging her son to take a more active role in the classroom, but explained that it might take a lot of time before he felt comfortable doing so. I found this to be true, but when I asked him to write or draw, he was able to share his thoughts. On the contrary, many students come to my class confident in their knowledge and their ability to share it with others. They benefit from the thoughtfulness of quieter kids who are slower to speak. In some cultures, girls are taught to take a passive role in learning and may be intimidated by the chatter and hands-on activities that often occur during inquiry science. It may be a good strategy to put these girls into a group together, so that they can practice speaking out in a safe setting. It can also be beneficial to encourage those who love to talk to take an active listening role and be patient and attentive when these more hesitant students speak up in a group.

In diverse classrooms, it is important that the teacher strive to understand the home cultures of the students. When we understand our students, it is easier to respect and embrace their differences. I find that sitting down and chatting informally with parents is the best way for me to do this. I discover so many interesting things that I probably never would have understood had I met them only at back-to-school night or briefly said hello outside at dismissal. A few years ago, I had a girl in my classroom who argued with everything I said. If I told her it was important to eat fruits and vegetables at lunch, she told me it was more important to eat protein since that is what made your muscles strong. If I told her that it was sunny outside, she made sure to inform me that it had been raining earlier that morning. By October, I had become quite frustrated with this student. When her mom came to school to have a beginning-of-the-year conference with me, I could tell right away that she was a strong woman who cared deeply about her family. She took over the conference, telling me stories about her family and how they had to leave her husband in Africa because he could not get the necessary clearance to come to the United States. She told me of her struggles in taking care of her kids and about the things she was doing to improve her life. She was going to school and working full-time, and she was somehow able to be at school to pick her kids up every day. She was strong. And she had taught her kids to be strong also. No wonder her daughter argued with me. She had a wonderful mother at home who was teaching her that you can change your future and don't have to accept the things that life hands you. She was being taught to be independent. This conversation with the mother changed my attitude toward this student immensely. I learned to ask her what she thought instead of telling her all the time. I asked her if she thought it would be a good idea to go outside and play even though it had been sprinkling earlier in the morning, and I let her decide what was important to eat at lunch. This was an easy change for me to make and didn't take away from my authority or change my role as a teacher, but it made my student feel valued and respected. I was able to be a better teacher to her instead of becoming frustrated with the way she did things.

In addition to understanding my students' home cultures, I have to be careful not to take anything for granted. Two of my Burmese students, for instance, who had come from refugee camps, had little knowledge of electricity. This made it difficult for them during our unit on energy to access some of the conversations that occurred. Our class still talked about power plants and electric lines running through the city, but I made sure to find lots of pictures and point out examples wherever I could. This lack of background knowledge didn't keep these students from making exciting discoveries and asking insightful questions. Toward the end of the unit one of these students, who was just starting to understand stored energy and solar power, asked if it was possible to recharge a battery by attaching it to a solar panel and leaving it in the sun. No one had ever asked me that question before. It made for some great explorations and classroom discussions.

Later I realized that it wasn't just my Burmese students who might have had trouble with this concept. After we wrapped up the unit, I drove a few of my students to an academic competition a few hours away from the school. I was driving, telling jokes, and singing with them when all of a sudden the students whipped out their cameras and started taking pictures right and left. It took me a second to figure out what had happened, but I eventually noticed that we were passing through a desert filled with windmills, and I realized that my students had never seen one before. I had seen many windmills on trips to my grandmother's house when growing up, so I figured that everyone else had a clear picture in their head when windmills were brought up in conversation.

For years I had always thought of my students as mini-versions of myself with a similar childhood and similar experiences growing up. But the truth is that they often come from places that are much different from ours. It is this diversity that makes a classroom sparkle as different perspectives, learning styles, cultures, and backgrounds come together.

8. Assessment Is More Than the "End-of-the-Year Chapter Test"

Just as the students' questions are going to help guide them throughout the inquiry process, the assessments you collect along the way will help you determine your next steps.

Your assessments determine where your students are, what they are curious about, what they are on the verge of understanding, or what they are having trouble with. When you know these things, it becomes easier to point your students in the right direction. As a teacher, you are constantly assessing. You are listening, reading student notebooks, watching, and noticing. You have a lot of information about your students! Figuring out where to go with all that information isn't always easy, but it gets easier the more you understand what your students do—and don't—understand.

This year, I began a scientific investigation by showing my class the salad I was going to eat for lunch and asking them where all the ingredients had come from. After discussing many of the items, my class began to focus on the carrots; they were very interested in where carrots came from since they had never noticed a carrot seed inside. Several students suggested that the seed was in there but that it was tiny and that we probably just don't notice it when we eat it. They asked if we could pull the carrots apart and look closely for a seed. I didn't let them destroy my lunch, but I did bring in some carrots the next day, and we spent some time pulling them apart and using a magnifying glass to see if we could find anything. I asked the students to put any seeds they found in a box in the front of the classroom. In twenty minutes there was a pile of tiny, seed-shaped carrot slivers in the box and many satisfied scientists in my classroom. They had solved the carrot mystery. The "seeds" were in the center of the carrot and needed to be carefully extracted, but they were in there and that must be how new carrots grew.

This experience provided a great assessment for me. Most of my class was satisfied with an incorrect notion of how carrots grew. I decided to ask how they knew they were seeds and if they could prove it. One student suggested planting the "seed" to see if it would grow, which was a great suggestion, but no one had any other ideas that would provide any results quickly. I suggested that we look inside some other seeds that I had to see what was inside. If we were familiar with seeds, maybe we would have some more evidence in support of their carrot conclusions. I pulled several large seeds out of the science kit given to me by my district and soaked them so that they would be easier to open. We pulled them apart slowly and noticed that there was something inside each one that looked like a tiny stem and a minuscule leaf. "Whoa!" I said. "Why would those be inside a seed?" After some talk, we decided that the carrot slivers were not, in fact, seeds, but the class was left stumped about where the seeds were. More assessment.

I decided to take a class trip out to our school garden where there were some tiny tomatoes growing inside the tiny flowers on the plant. We observed the tomatoes, talked about where tomato seeds were, and determined that some fruits grow out of flowers.

"Is there a carrot fruit?" asked one of the students tentatively. A few students giggled, but then the idea caught on, and hands shot up to ask me if they could use Google to find out what the entire carrot plant looked like. They wanted to know if it had flowers and what was inside them. I carefully watched and listened to these independent investigations occurring in my classroom and determined that we were ready to start thinking more about plant cycles. I knew where to go.

My class did end up taking a test at the end of the unit, but this is not where I gleaned most of my information about their understanding. To me, this test was like the survey they give you at the end of a stay on a cruise ship. It asks you how your trip was, but it is too late to fix anything for passengers. It's great for future guests, since changes can be put into place for next time. But for those enthusiastic patrons who were eager to get more time to water-ski, an opportunity was missed.

9. The Science Curriculum Can't Drive the Inquiry Process

I enjoy cooking, but I am definitely not a chef! I need to follow a recipe—a specific recipe. In fact, it is a great pet peeve of mine when I read a recipe that includes the words *to taste*. "Salt and pepper *to taste*." Or "chili powder *to taste*." Why doesn't it just tell me how many teaspoons of salt to put in? I need the exact amount. My taste buds haven't been trained to determine how much salt is tasty and how much is overkill until it's too late. And I love chili pepper, so I put in a lot and later realize that my "to taste" amount made my dish so spicy that my guests had to consume twelve glasses of water just to politely nibble away half the casserole I served them.

No, I am not a chef. Chefs dip a spoon into the soup pot, taste it, and determine that "it needs a bit more oregano." Chefs taste a sauce they have made, wonder what is missing, and then remake the sauce until it is just right. I was recently talking to a colleague who told me that after about fifteen attempts, he had almost re-created his father's potato salad recipe. Now, *he's* a chef! If I wanted tasty potato salad, I would Google a recipe, read all the comments, and make the one with the highest ratings. Then I would evaluate it with my two-point test: I either like it or it's gross, in which case I would throw away the recipe.

Science curriculums, like cookbooks, often include the exact procedures for students to follow so that they end up with perfect conclusions. They walk you through the science that someone else has already done. All of the "tasting" and testing and fixing have been taken care of.

Inquiry happens when a student has a question and hunts for the answer. Experiments are done in a quest to confirm a hypothesis, not because it is Day 5 and an experiment is required.

A few years ago, my class was grappling with someone's idea that the sun moved around the earth. He said, "I know it moves, because I have noticed that my shadow is in different places throughout the day." (It may be important to point out that this idea is scientifically incorrect, but the student had evidence for this common misconception, so his idea was worth exploring.)

"It is?" another classmate responded. "Our shadow moves?"

"I think so," the student answered back. "Could we go outside and check?"

"Sure," I answered. "How will we do that?"

"We could go out now and trace our shadows, and then go out again a little later and see if they have moved."

I loved this suggestion. The student described a wonderful procedure that would actually provide insight into the investigation, *and*, coincidentally, this exact experiment was included in my science curriculum. In fact, I had large yellow chalk for tracing in the large kit of materials.

It was in the curriculum because it was a wonderful activity. It had been carefully thought out and perfectly placed in a sequence of activities that would build the students' understanding of the earth and the sun. My class didn't follow that sequence, but we ended up doing many of the activities because they really made sense. The biggest difference was that it was the students' inquiry that was driving the activities, not the sequence in the teacher's manual.

Science curriculums or kit-based science activities hold a wealth of information and a plethora of wonderful activities. Is it possible to use these and teach inquiry-based science? Yes! In *Beyond the Science Kit: Inquiry in Action*, Wendy Saul and Jeanne Reardon (1996) stress the need to make science activities real, rigorous, and relevant. The shadow-tracing activity was all of those since the students were investigating an authentic question that they were in charge of. The science belongs to the students. The kit is a tool that can be used when the need arises rather than a list of recipes for the students to follow.

10. The Way We Communicate with Students Makes a Difference

As a teacher, you probably spend a large portion of the day talking, and what you say really matters, especially in inquiry science. Carefully chosen words have the power to get your entire class participating. At the same time, the wrong words have the potential to shut down the thinking of many of your students. I want my students to feel comfortable and daring during science time. I want them to take a risk and propose an idea that is "out there" but makes people think. I want them to feel safe and trust that no matter what they say, I will still think they're smart. I want all these things for my classroom, so I have learned to choose my words wisely.

You see, everything I say, and even the things I don't say, communicates a message to students that tells them whether or not it is okay to proceed. My words are just as important as home life, parent support, motivation, and background knowledge. They can determine the success or failure of my students during inquiry science.

Let's take a look at some of the things teachers have said during an investigation of how the sun, moon, and earth work in the solar system (see Figure 2.3). The students had noticed that the moon appears in several different shapes at night. One student suggested that there are several different moons, and that when the earth spins, a different moon is visible on

Type of Teacher Response	Example of the Teacher's Actual Words	Potential Effect These Words Have on Student Learning
Denying	Well, no, not really. Does anyone else have any ideas?	The student who contributed the response feels embarrassed at having given an incorrect answer, which halts his thinking about the moon. Next time a question is asked, this student will think twice before contributing and may feel anxious about being incorrect again. Eventually this student may stop contributing to class conversations. The rest of the students know that you hold the right answer and may be reluctant to speak unless they are sure they know it.
Ignoring	Okay. How about someone else?	The student who contributed the answer feels that his idea was not good enough to merit a response. This may affect future participation and can contribute to an unhealthy disposition about science. She no longer feels that she is a smart scientist.
Providing a Counterargument	That would mean that people in different parts of the world see different moons than we do. Actually, people in different parts of the earth see the same moon shape.	This response may prompt some more thinking from some students since they will want to figure out the answer to the counterargument you provided. However, some students may think that their contributions are meaningless since you seem to have the right answer and may argue with anything that is incorrect.
Validating and Pondering	Hmmm . . . that's an interesting idea. Let's think more about that. So are you saying that there are many moons and that the one we see depends on where the earth is on its rotation? Do you want to come up and draw what that would look like?	The student thinks that his contribution was helpful and may lead the class to a scientific discovery. The rest of the class begins to think about this idea since you have validated it. Students may come up with questions or counterarguments on their own. "Wait a minute . . . That would mean that the whole world saw the moon at the same time. I know that it is nighttime in China right now, so that can't be." The discussion progresses and other students join in to solve the problem.

Figure 2.3 • Teacher Responses to Incorrect Answers

a different night. This is scientifically incorrect, but what is said in response to the comment is extremely important.

Your words are also important when a student gives a response that is scientifically accurate. In a group of students trying to sort different objects into the appropriate states of matter, a student may suggest that sand is a solid. Following are some teacher responses and the potential effects the words have on student learning (see Figure 2.4).

When moderating scientific discussions, it is important to think about the effect your words will have on the class. The best responses are those that encourage students to keep thinking and to defend their answers with viable arguments. Pay attention and take note of what happens with each student after you share a response. Choosing the right words takes practice, but the work is worth it. It will pay off in students who are confident and comfortable contributing even when they aren't positive their answer is correct.

Type of Response	Example of Actual Words	Potential Effect on Student Learning
Confirming	Yes! You are right. Sand is a solid.	The student who answered the questions feels successful. The rest of the class may be disappointed that they did not have a chance to answer since they also were correct. The class stops thinking about sand and waits for the teacher to ask another question.
Confirm and ask for more.	Yes! You are right. How do you know sand is a solid?	The student who answered the question may or may not be able to communicate his reasoning. The rest of the class may not listen attentively to the explanation because the teacher has already confirmed that the answer was correct.
Probing	Can you tell us why you think sand is a solid?	The student must defend his thinking. Since this is often difficult to do, other students may join in and help him articulate it. Additionally, there may be some children who disagree and want to propose a different argument. "Wait a second. I can pour sand, and it makes a big mess, kind of like water. I think it is a liquid." The students are engaged in the process of coming to consensus and defending their thinking.

Figure 2.4 • Teacher Responses to Correct Answers

The way we communicate with students has an effect on whether conversations during inquiry science are productive or not. In their book *Classroom Discussions: Seeing Math Discourse in Action*, Suzanne Chapin, Catherine O'Connor, and Nancy C. Anderson (2011) describe several important talk moves that help students and teachers master the art of productive talk in the classroom.

Strategy: Say More

Example: *"Can you say more about that, Amanda?"*

This strategy helps a teacher who has heard what a student has shared but has not understood the content of what he or she has said. The strategy can also be useful when a student's idea is not sufficiently supported by evidence. For example, when I was investigating light with my students, I asked the class where rainbows come from. "From raindrops," several students exclaimed. This response did little to explain the scientific reasons rainbows can be formed, so I chose one of the students who offered that explanation and asked him to say more about the idea. After some think time, the student continued. "Well, the water has colors in it, and when the light falls through it, the colors . . . show up out of the water." I wondered about his statement that the water has colors in it, so I asked him to tell me more about them. He continued, "You know, like the ocean is blue, or sometimes I see different colors in the puddles on the ground after it rains. One time, I saw an entire rainbow in a puddle underneath my car." This idea is incorrect, but the student had given the entire class something to think about. However, to make sure that I understood exactly what he was saying, and so that the rest of the students understood as well, I employed another talk move: revoicing.

Strategy: Revoicing

Example: *"So you're saying that water has the colors of the rainbow inside it and when light passes through the water, we can see the colors?"*

By revoicing what the student said, my intention was not to put words in his mouth or to criticize his answer in any way. Rather, I revoiced his idea to help him clarify his words so that other students understood exactly what he was saying. This gave all the students an entry point into the investigation. It gave them a place to start thinking.

Strategy: Asking Students to Restate Someone Else's Idea

Example: *"Can someone repeat what Juan said in your own words?"*

Asking students to restate someone else's idea helps them "orient to the thinking of others" and encourages active listening. When students repeat others' words, they are making sure they have heard each other, a vital step before they evaluate each other's ideas. This can also be a useful step for English language learners, who can greatly benefit from hearing the same idea repeated several times. I like to use this move when a student has shared something important (whether scientifically correct or incorrect) or something that might help move the conversation forward. In our discussion of rainbows, one student shared that he had seen rainbows indoors although he knew there was no rain inside. "You know what?" I said. "I've noticed that too. Can anyone repeat what he just said?"

Strategy: Pressing for Reasoning

Example: *"You said you think the light will be red, but why do you think that?"*

In order to have productive, scientific talk, it is important to encourage students to deepen their reasoning and back up their claims with evidence or an explanation. For example, as students in my class were investigating light, I asked them what color the light would be if I shined a flashlight through a red gel. Most agreed that it would be red. When I asked them to explain why, several said that they had seen this before when looking through bottles or other translucent materials of different colors. I then shined the light through the red gel and allowed the students to see the red light that appeared on the wall behind them. Next, I placed a blue gel behind the red and asked what color the light would be when shining it through both gels. Several students agreed on purple. When I pressed for reasoning, someone said that because red and blue paint make purple, the light traveling through the gels would mix as well. It was important that students formulated and shared their reasoning so that when they discovered that the light was not in fact purple, but was completely gone, they could go back to their explanation to revise it so that it made sense with what they had just seen.

Maybe the gel was too thick, so the light could not pass through, they reasoned.

Maybe it's because it is dark blue. Can we try a lighter blue?

What if we switch the order of the gels?

When students are asked to back up their ideas with evidence or reasoning, they move beyond what they see and try to make sense of why they see them. This is a key skill that scientists use in their work.

Strategy: Asking Students to Apply Their Own Reasoning to Someone Else's Idea

Example: *"Do you agree or disagree, and why?"*

Asking students if they agree or disagree with another student's thinking encourages everyone to evaluate what was said and provide further reasoning for its accuracy or inaccuracy. The responsibility for the evaluation of ideas is no longer entirely on the teacher's shoulders. Each student in the class gets a shot at deciding what is true. For example, when a student shared that rainbows are formed when light travels through colored water, another student offered a counterargument right away. This student no longer needed to be asked whether or not he agreed and why; he did that thinking on his own. However, at times, it is helpful for the teacher to ask the entire class if they agree or disagree, and why. This way all the students are in direct contact with the reasoning of their peers.

Strategy: Prompting Students for More Participation

Example: *"Who would like to add to what Cesar just said?"*

Asking students to add to the ideas of others can also help them engage in each other's thinking. For a student to add on, he must first understand what was said and the reasoning behind it so that he may add his own reasoning. When I asked students if anyone wanted to add to the idea that rainbows appear after light passes through colored water, another student agreed and added that she often saw rainbows when the sprinklers were on at her apartment complex.

Strategy: Using Wait Time

Example: *"Take your time . . . we'll wait . . ."*

The final talk move is essential to all the others: wait time. This move lets students know that what they have to say is valuable and worth waiting for. It is important that teachers hold their tongue and remain silent for at least five seconds to allow students to formulate their ideas into a comprehensible statement that others can understand. This is especially important for English language learners, who may need to translate your question into their native language and then back into English, or may simply need more time to come up with the right words to say. Giving students adequate wait time helps them feel less anxious about participating in conversations.

USING THE GUIDING PRINCIPLES TO DESIGN EFFECTIVE LEARNING ENVIRONMENTS

In *How People Learn: Brain, Mind, Experience, and School* (Bransford, Brown, and Cocking 2000), the National Research Council describes effective learning environments as centered on four key components: learner, knowledge, assessment, and community. Learner-centered classrooms build on the knowledge that students bring to the learning situation and recognize that disequilibrium and naïve conceptions are a natural part of the learning process and are important starting places for sense making. Knowledge-centered classrooms focus on big ideas, important concepts, and making connections rather than on lecturing, rote learning, and memorization. Assessment-centered classrooms are ones where teachers attempt to make students' thinking visible so that ideas can be discussed, argued, debated, and clarified. And finally, community-centered classrooms are places where learning with understanding is valued and where students are encouraged "to explore what they do not understand." The principles outlined in this chapter are intended to not only instill a sense of excitement about teaching inquiry science, but also to guide us as we strive to improve our instruction and design science-learning environments that are effective for all students, especially those who have been underserved by our education system.

CHAPTER 3

MANAGING THE DIVERSE CLASSROOM DURING INQUIRY SCIENCE

Managing a classroom can be one of the most difficult challenges teachers face. This is especially true when teaching inquiry science in diverse classrooms. Teaching inquiry in the manner that we propose in this book requires teachers to give up some of the control they are accustomed to having. They hand over the thinking, experimenting, and most of the talking to the students. During inquiry science, students are moving about, talking, listening to one another, working in groups, and using materials. All of this activity has the potential to facilitate a lot of learning, but it can also pose many management challenges. The most creative lessons or investigations are worthless if students are ignoring directions, misbehaving, using materials inappropriately, being unsafe, or acting in a disrespectful manner.

We have learned a great deal from the Responsive Classroom approach to classroom management (www.responsiveclassroom.org). This approach sees the social and academic curriculum as intertwined, one affecting the other. When students are respected, and explicitly taught how to practice self-control and manage their own behaviors, they begin to learn more and feel a sense of empowerment. This sense of empowerment is especially important for students who have traditionally been underserved by our educational system. A teacher can be strict, consistent, and explicit and still treat students with respect and give them a voice.

In this chapter, Sharon shares ten keys to managing the diverse classroom during inquiry science. She draws upon her many years of experience teaching science at a school with a very diverse student population, and she is guided by many of the principles from the Responsive Classroom approach. Sharon's advice focuses on proactive practices that are aimed at developing independent, responsible, and respectful young scientists.

TEN KEYS TO MANAGING THE DIVERSE CLASSROOM DURING INQUIRY

The following research-based suggestions are essential for building a classroom culture that supports inquiry.

1. Create a Safe Environment for Learning

A few years ago, I was invited to participate in a curriculum opinion session with a group of teachers in my city. Before we began the session, we shared our names and the grade and school in which we taught. Then we jumped into a lengthy conversation about a new math curriculum that was going to be offered up to the state for approval. The moderator wanted to know which parts we liked and didn't like and if we thought it would promote student success.

I didn't love the curriculum, despite the fact that every other teacher on the panel thought it was great. Most of the teachers discussed how the curriculum had many resources that would be useful for teachers and provided many models that would help deepen students' understanding. I thought the materials were teacher-centered and didn't provide students with many chances to practice critical thinking, but I remained silent throughout most of the conversation. I am usually confident in my opinions and comfortable sharing them, but in this situation, I was terrified of going against the flow. Toward the end of the session, I did offer one opinion and instantly regretted it. One other participant quickly interrupted me to counter my ideas, and at the same time, two others began whispering to each other across the table. The moderator moved right past my comment and asked a new question. Needless to say, I didn't offer any more opinions, and I didn't even hear what the other participants had to say. I focused on trying to disappear.

Little was done in this situation to create an environment in which it was safe for the participants to share. And because of this, I missed an opportunity to learn from the other participants, and everyone involved missed a chance to learn from me. I wish the moderator had done more to ensure that everyone who wanted to share felt comfortable doing so.

Although this was one uncomfortable day for me, it would be a tragedy for a student to spend an entire year feeling like I did. And it would be horrible to miss out on all of a student's good thoughts because he or she did not feel safe. For this reason, it is extremely important that teachers work hard to create a safe environment where students feel comfortable sharing and taking risks. Too often teachers work on building a community of learners at the beginning of the year and then let that fall to the wayside once they begin rigorous instruction. Students need us to help build a classroom community throughout the year. Here are several ways to work on building a safe classroom environment.

Build Familiarity

Help your students get to know each other. Allow them to share stories about their lives and cultures so that they can appreciate the diversity they have among them. Encourage kids to share their struggles and celebrate accomplishments together. When they truly understand each other, they develop empathy. When students can put themselves in each other's shoes, they are more likely to think about how their actions might affect someone else.

Create a Culture of Kindness

Model the Golden Rule to your students. Talk to them the way you want them to talk to each other. If you want kids to respect each other, respect them, especially when you discipline them. Be a leader of kindness, and kids will want to jump on your bandwagon.

Be an Active Listener

Your students want to be just like you, and they will do what you do. If you want students to listen to each other, listen to them. When it's Monday morning and a student is excitedly telling you every single detail about her trip to the Laundromat last Saturday, listen and engage in the conversation. Ask a question or share a similar anecdote. Kids are smart, and they know that when you nod your head and say, "Cool," you aren't really paying attention. Additionally, when you ask the class a question and hear an off-the-wall answer, resist the urge to laugh or to say something that moves the conversation in a different direction. This lets the responder and the rest of the class know that you did not value what he or she had to say. Instead, take a moment to ponder what the student said. Ask a question about it, or probe for some clarification. Sometimes a simple "What did you mean?" will prompt a student to expand his or her thoughts enough for everyone to realize that there actually was some merit in what was said in the first place.

Get Your Hands Dirty

When students are unkind to each other or do something that may cause another student to feel that what he or she has to say is not good enough, get in there and help the kids problem solve. Too often teachers end the situation by removing the offender or by assessing some form of discipline, but this does little to help students learn how to permanently change their behavior. Instead, engage the offender in a conversation that helps him realize how his actions might have made the other student feel. Ask him to verbalize the consequences of his unkind remarks. Help him empathize and realize (ideally) that he doesn't actually want to hurt his classmate. This will help the student think before acting (or speaking) next time.

Get Off the Stage

It's hard to share when you feel like someone else knows all the right answers and is judging everything you say. Kids think you know everything. And not only do students think you know everything, but your presence is a powerful one. Remember how hard it was for Dorothy to talk to the great and all-powerful Oz? For kids, teachers are the all-knowing beings who rule over their classroom. They may know we're "good," but we can be intimidating sometimes. So instead of standing in front of the class during discussions, grab a stool and put yourself closer to their level. Join them! (See Figure 3.1.) When you make yourself smaller (less tall), kids feel empowered to share and try out ideas, and they don't feel quite as nervous about that "all-knowing being" telling them they are wrong.

Figure 3.1
Sharon joins
the students as
they work.

Handle Interruptions Fairly

Have you ever noticed how much adults interrupt each other in normal conversations? I, for one, know that I am a huge offender. When someone says something I relate to, my immediate impulse is to join in the conversation. Most adults are skilled at pausing their stories or sentences to accommodate interruptions, and they often appreciate them. It's how we show each other that we are really listening and that we care about and relate to what is being said. I hate it when my friends stare at me silently while I talk. Yet this is often what we expect of our students: one person talks and everyone else is silent until they are finished. Take a second to really listen to your students when they interrupt. More often than not they are doing the same thing adults do during most conversations: they are agreeing with you, connecting with what you're saying, or wondering about something related to your topic. Instead of punishing students for interrupting, teach them how to maneuver through conversations like adults do. When two students are talking at once, show them that nobody can really listen to either one of them, so one of them should take a break until the other finishes. In my classroom, I am delighted when a student who has been interrupted stops to listen to the offender before continuing. Usually this is a cue to the interrupter that they had better make it quick and go back to listening. For the times when the kids need more help than that, be more direct. You might say, "I really want to hear what you have to say, but I wasn't finished listening to _____." This lets both students know that what they have to say is important and that you really want to hear them.

2. Set Up a Morning Meeting

It's Friday at 8:45 and my class is getting ready to leave for a field trip. The bus leaves at 9:00, and we are in a mad rush to get breakfast cleaned up, get homework turned in, take attendance, find our field trip buddies, and make name tags. I ask everyone to get everything together and line up next to their buddy while I take attendance. All of a sudden I hear a chorus of students all complaining about the same thing. "Aren't we going to have a morning meeting? Can we just have a short one?"

We don't have time. We barely have time to get out the door, but I can't say no. This is how my students connect to each other at the beginning of every day. It's how they get their day going in the right direction, and if it doesn't happen, it just doesn't feel right.

I know that building and maintaining a community of learners is an important part of creating a safe environment where students are willing to take risks academically. Morning meeting (Figure 3.2) is a time each morning when we focus on building togetherness, feeling safe, and understanding each other.

In *The Morning Meeting Book*, Roxann Kriete writes about the importance of teaching and practicing social skills with your students: "A person who can listen well, who can frame a good question and has the assertiveness to pose it, who can examine a situation from a number of perspectives will be a strong learner. All those skills—skills essential to academic

Figure 3.2
Morning
Meeting

achievement—must be modeled, experienced, practiced, extended, and refined in the context of social interaction. Morning Meeting is a forum in which that happens" (2002, 8–9). These are skills I need my students to have and feel comfortable with in inquiry science! For this reason, I have found that morning meeting is essential in my classroom.

Our meeting begins with a greeting. The children sit in a circle, and every person acknowledges the others by name. Students can choose from a variety of greetings and like to find new ways to say "good morning" in different languages.

After we greet each other, there is a time for students to share what is on their minds or anything that they need to tell the rest of the class before the day begins. Sometimes students tell about a fun activity that happened the night before. Sometimes the sharing is much more serious. The kids may tell about family issues or things that are bothering them in the classroom. The kids know that this is a time we can problem solve, so if someone hurt your feelings yesterday at recess, morning meeting is a good time to bring it up. Kids practice listening to each other, trying to understand each other's feelings and figuring out how they can make things right. Sometimes, it takes a while to teach students how to listen purposefully, but I find that when we practice this often, the kids learn to have talks like these independently and more problems get solved without my help. And, when they learn to listen to each other, their listening spills over into my science time! Morning meeting is also a great time for teachers to bring up things that are bothering them about student behavior, routines and procedures, or student work. Maybe you have noticed that during science time, many kids are interrupting each other. Morning meeting allows you to have a brainstorming session about how to solve the problem. Kids might suggest choosing a student to be the "interrupting monitor" and decide who will talk first and who should wait until the speaker is finished, or they may decide they can work on the problem independently by being purposeful about pausing when they notice two people talking at once. Morning meeting conversations are useful for problem solving because when the students come up with solutions, they are more likely to help each other stick to them.

We always end the morning meeting with a shared activity that brings everyone together again. We might play a short game, sing a song, or read one of our class poems together.

Morning meeting takes a diverse classroom of students and teachers and unites them into one close-knit group who trust and respect each other. Students from different cultures learn about and start to feel comfortable with the way that Americans greet each other on a day-to-day basis, and they can learn about and appreciate each other's cultures. Students can also learn to appreciate each other's differences. Recently, my class used a chunk of morning meeting time to understand autism, so that they could be more empathetic toward one of their classmates.

English language learners benefit from morning meeting as well. These students may start off as quiet observers, but they usually join in once they realize it is a safe space to speak. It doesn't take long, since morning meeting gives these students an authentic reason to want to talk. They may want to share about something going on that is important to them, but when you notice students who are still reluctant to speak after quite some time, try giving them something to talk about. Morning meeting is a great time for students to share what they worked on in their science notebooks, or the question that they thought of while they were at the grocery store the night before. You may find that it is helpful to have students share in pairs first, so that ELL students have time to practice their language with one person before they report to the class.

3. Let Students Have a Say in Creating Rules and Procedures

To make inquiry science successful in your classroom, you will want your students to respect and internalize the classroom rules. In *Rules in School*, Brady, Forton, Porter, and Wood (2011) suggest creating rules with your students so that they take ownership of them. To do this, the class starts by sharing their hopes and dreams for the year. They may share what they would like to learn or accomplish, which often starts with the teacher sharing her hopes and dreams. She may say, "I hope that we will all be able to listen to each other and use kindness when we talk to each other." Then, a list of rules is co-created that will help the class achieve all of their dreams. For instance, a student who desires to become a better reader may create the rule that everyone should work hard during independent reading. A student who wants to do lots of science experiments during class may suggest that the class use materials appropriately. Once a long list of rules has been created, the class works together to combine the rules into three to five principles that seem to cover them all (see Figure 3.3). Your final rules may be to respect yourself and others, respect the classroom, and respect your time. Or, take care of others, take care of yourself, and take care of our school.

Once your rules have been created, your students will need help knowing how to apply them during science time. Have conversations with them about what each rule will look like. You might say, "We agreed that we would all respect each other. What can we do while we are involved in a

Figure 3.3
Involve
students in
creating class
rules.

class discussion to make sure that happens?" Or, "We agreed that it is important to take care of ourselves. How will we show that we are doing this as we start our work today?" This way, students know that they need to get started quickly and work without wasting time because they created and truly understand the rule.

4. Create a Disciplinary System That Makes Sense

Recently, my class was engaged in an investigation about what happens to the properties of matter when they are mixed, and they were using vinegar and baking soda to explore. I opened the bottle of vinegar and let the students smell it before we began. We all agreed it smelled pretty bad and had a conversation about how we wouldn't want our classroom to smell that way after our investigation was over. We brainstormed some rules for using the vinegar carefully so that it wouldn't spill, and the kids began their investigations. It took only a few minutes for one of the groups to knock their vinegar over and spill it all over the floor because they were acting silly. The members of the group gasped and turned to look at my reaction. A few pointed at the student who did the spilling, as if to indicate blame. They were ready to be scolded. However, the natural consequence the students experienced did much more to teach them about responsibility than scolding them would. A few had spots of vinegar on their clothes, which caused the unpleasant smell to travel with them for the rest of the day. The others could smell it in the classroom until the next day. They all immediately knew why it was important to be careful. Although I was frustrated by the smell, I held back my lecture, because I knew that the lesson had already been learned. The students wiped up the mess, and we continued with our investigation.

Sometimes, it is tempting to hand out consequences that aren't very natural. If students talk out of turn too many times, they lose part of their recess, or if they use a material for something it wasn't intended for, they get their name put up on the board. These types of punishments don't seem to help students learn why it is important to change their behavior next time. The authors of *Rules in School* describe their goals in responding to rule breaking. They are to help students learn from their mistakes and learn how to fix them while maintaining a calm and orderly classroom. They suggest using logical consequences, which are relevant, realistic, and respectful when students break the rules (Brady, Forton, and Porter 2011). For instance, a student who has used his time to talk about his plans for recess instead of recording his findings in his science notebook would need to sit somewhere away from the group so that he could work without distraction. Similarly, a group of students who are fighting over materials being used in an investigation would lose the privilege of using those materials for a period of time. Or, if a student is acting silly during a class discussion, he or she may need to take a break from the group to regain control.

Students want to be part of the group, and they want to do what everyone else is doing. When they can't, they learn to change their behavior so that they can next time. A natural consequence is enough to learn a lesson, and often, no scolding is required.

When you're teaching inquiry science, you'll want to have a well-thought-out disciplinary system. Behavior issues can distract from learning time and take away from the flow of a good conversation, argument, or experiment. However, when consequences don't make sense, students learn that they need to improve their behavior to avoid punishment. If we really want them to learn a lesson that lasts, we have to use consequences that make sense.

5. Set Boundaries

I find that science is a lot more fun when I leave a little space for students to be who they are. Some of the students in my diverse classroom are "slow cookers" and have to let ideas stew in their brains for quite some time before they say anything. Others love to talk right from the get-go and often interrupt because they are excited. Some love to question others, and some are overly skeptical. Some love to write in their notebook, whereas others would rather talk it out with a partner. There is a lot of room to be yourself in an inquiry science classroom, but clear boundaries need to be set.

Students know that there are different ways to be a part of the class and participate. At times they can sit quietly and think. Other times, debating politely is okay. Getting up without permission to grab their notebook and write down a thought is even acceptable, but everyone needs to participate in some way. Passive learning is unacceptable in the inquiry science classroom, and the students know that this rule is clear. I make sure it is clear by using a firm voice when I remind students and by following through with natural consequences if I notice students who are not participating. I may have a child move to the front of the group to be free of distractions or I may create an assigned seat away from the child's friends. Sometimes it is necessary to conference with the student at a different time to find out what the problem is and make sure my expectations are known.

During one science conversation that my students were having, I noticed two girls whispering to each other in the back. My hope was that they were having an impromptu partner talk about what they wanted to add to the conversation. Although their behavior wasn't exactly polite, I was understanding with these girls because they are both in the beginning stage of learning English and I sympathized with their need to practice before sharing with the class. However, upon further investigation, I found that in actuality, they were planning a trip to visit each other's houses and were exchanging phone numbers to make this possible. Although these students were usually well-behaved learners in my classroom, I dismissed them from the group right away and let them know that I wouldn't tolerate such conversations. The message was clear to the girls, who were eager to rejoin the group, as well as to the rest of the class, who realized that this was a clear rule for all students. Students need to know what their boundaries are in order to stay away from them.

6. Set Up Social Conferences

I'll never forget the day my class was having a discussion about where carrots come from and a student made barking noises every time someone began a sentence. It was horribly disruptive. No one could talk, we couldn't hear each other, and the students couldn't control their laughter each time a new bark was released. That, however, is not why this situation is ingrained in my memory. I'll always remember how I handled this situation, and to this day, I wish I'd dealt with it differently.

I tried to ignore this student for quite some time and asked the class to ignore him also, hoping the behavior would stop. I shot several "I'm getting very annoyed" looks across the classroom. I moved the student to a new seat, and I asked him to take a break in the cooling-off area. The barking continued, and I gave the student an ultimatum. "Either you stop barking right now or you can bark in the principal's office. The next time I hear any dog noises from you, you can march right down and explain how rude your behavior has been." I heard the next *ruff* and told the student he needed to leave. The student became very upset. He cried loudly and begged not to go. He threw books at other children and ran around the classroom, baiting me into a game of cat and mouse. Needless to say, our science time was over.

If I could repeat this situation, I would invite the student into a social conference. Conferences like these invite the child into a conversation about his actions and ask that he take accountability for them in a way that is productive for everyone involved. I wish I would have talked with this student privately and asked him about his behavior—if he was feeling all right, or if there was a specific reason he was barking. We could have come up with a solution together so that neither of us had to get upset. The conversation might have gone something like this:

> **Me:** I notice that you're really having trouble concentrating right now.
>
> **Student:** Yup, I'm barking.
>
> **Me:** Your behavior is making it hard for me and the other students to concentrate. Is there a reason it is so hard for you today?
>
> **Student:** During lunch, I was thinking about how my mom didn't pay attention to me last night. She was too busy with my baby brother. It's making me upset.
>
> **Me:** Hmm, I can see why that would make you upset. Would you like to take a break so that you can calm down?
>
> **Student:** Can I write my mom a letter so that she can read it after school?
>
> **Me:** That sounds like a great idea. I can't wait for you to join us again when you are finished.

Social conferences allow you and the student to find solutions to behavioral problems in a private, safe setting. Now that I regularly set up social conferences in my classroom, the students often ask for one themselves, and they have even held their own conferences with other students with whom they have had conflicts. The time spent setting up these conferences has definitely paid off since the students know that their feelings matter and will be heard. Behavioral problems are usually fixed very quickly.

7. Foster Healthy Dispositions Toward Science

People often ask me how I can get twenty-four nine-year-olds to sit on the floor for more than an hour and discuss one person's idea and then be excited about coming back the next day and continuing the conversation. My answer is always the same. They do it because they love it. My students love science time, they feel like they are good at it, and they really believe that if they persevere in solving a problem, they can come up with some wonderful scientific discoveries. They are curious, and they think their discussions are purposeful and actually leading them to the discovery they want. A good disposition is essential for classroom management since students are less likely to display unwanted behaviors when they love what they are doing. But where do healthy dispositions come from?

I certainly didn't have one when I was a child. For me, science was hard, and I didn't get it. I could follow the directions on a lab just fine and could read whatever you put before me, but did I love it? Not really. Did I try hard to understand what I was doing? Absolutely not. Science just wasn't my thing, and that was okay.

Now, as a teacher, my entire disposition toward science has changed: you can often find me pondering something scientific at a dinner party or a baseball game. I love asking questions and thinking with friends about how to answer them. You see, a few years ago, someone I admired and respected helped me change my disposition toward science. He engaged me with riveting questions and showed a genuine interest in my answers. He listened to and wrote down the things I said. And I will never forget the moment when one of the smartest people I knew told me that I was good at science. I had never been told that in my life! The best part was that I knew he really meant it, because I *felt* good at it. At that moment, my love of science grew, and so did my tolerance for sticking with it and thinking something through until it made sense.

I grew to love science and have a desire to understand it when it became less about memorizing facts and following procedures and more about my ability to think about and make sense of the world. When I was told (and shown) that my contributions were valuable, my curiosity and perseverance grew, and now when I read a textbook, I work hard to understand what I am reading.

It's my goal to share this love for science with my students. I make it a point to listen to and write down what they are saying. I get excited about ideas they are excited about. I am curious when they are curious. I let them try things and come up with new ideas. I tell them often that they are good at science. And you know what? It really works. Many students look at the schedule first thing in the morning and give a little cheer when they notice that science is on it. They groan when we have to quit, and they talk about science at recess. I even notice them sneaking out their science books when they are supposed to be working on something else. Student behavior is at its best during science time. Students with too much energy quickly become engaged when given a real problem that's not easy to solve, language learners strive to speak more because they have something real that they want to say, and the student who sits quietly and waits to hear the right answer wakes up because she realizes that it is up to her to determine what is really correct.

While working with a fifth-grade class (see Chapter 5), I noticed that one student grabbed a paper out of a classmate's hand and loudly berated her for mixing up his name with that of another student. I quickly let the student know that his behavior was unacceptable and asked him to apologize, but I made it a point to go and have a conversation with him once the class had started working. I asked him what was wrong, and although he told me that everything was fine, I knew that he was having an extremely rough day. He was disrespectful and reluctant to get to work. I sat with him for a second and asked him about the question and hypothesis he had created. I noticed his demeanor change as I showed interest in his thoughts and authentic curiosity in following up on his experiment. After a while, he went happily to work with a great attitude, and was excited to share his findings at the end of class. His disposition toward science really mattered. When he knew that his ideas and contributions were valued, he improved his behavior drastically.

8. *Manage Materials Effectively*

A good science experiment often means a messy one, and when kids are investigating, you don't know exactly what is going to happen. Substances spill, pieces break, kids could even end up getting hurt. You can never be too explicit when you are managing materials, and it is worth it to spend some time setting up expectations before you turn the kids loose to explore. Going to be working with bags of dirt? Take some time to imagine what could happen when groups of kids reach into the bag to scoop out soil and put it into plastic cups, and give the class some very specific directions to make sure that you never see that situation come to life. Are you working with something that gets hot? Make sure you point out the dangers, and clearly state how to avoid them.

It's important that all the students are tuned in while you are stating expectations. This is not the time for your whimsical student in the back to start daydreaming. Let the students know that you mean business and that there are no chances when it comes to these rules. Sometimes, it is even a good idea to role-play your expectations so that kids can see exactly what is expected of them. Make sure everyone understands the directions before you let them touch the materials (see Figure 3.4). You can have the whole class do a choral repeat of the directions or ask specific students what the different parts of the directions were. Have the kids practice until you think it is overkill, and then do it a couple more times. It may seem tedious, but you want the class to know that this is important and that you mean business.

Figure 3.4
Managing
materials is key
to making
inquiry science
run smoothly.

As the students are working, it is important to act when you notice that someone is not following the directions. If you asked that their cups of dirt always remain in the center of the table so that they aren't spilled on the floor and you notice that one group's cups are heading toward the table edge, remove the group from the activity for a short period of time. Tell them what you're seeing and have them sit in an area of the room away from the science investigation. Leave them alone for a minute or two so that they have time to process what caused them to be over there. After a short time, go talk to the offenders. Make sure they know what they did wrong and that they understand how they need to handle the materials when they return to their project. I usually let them know that next time it happens, they will be permanently removed from the activity. Your follow-through is what lets kids know whether they should trust what you say. If you give too many chances, the students know that they can make a few mistakes, and they are not as careful to follow the rules the first time. If you gave precise directions, make sure that you are careful with your follow-through. The students will know that you mean what you say and that they had better listen carefully the first time.

9. Facilitate Group Work

Group work can be a vital component in an inquiry-based classroom. It encourages students to be active and involved learners, strengthens their communication skills, and helps them engage in problem solving and critical thinking. However, it takes some good facilitating to get groups to work together well.

If possible, think about the size of the groups and who will be in each one beforehand. Sometimes it's fine for students to pick their own groups, and they will often choose their friends to work with at first. However, after group work becomes more familiar to them, they tend to choose students with whom they work well and who are at their level of thinking and problem solving (see Figure 3.5). Sometimes you *will* want to choose who is in each group so that you can control the dynamics. You may want to put students together by language ability so that you can ensure that a native English speaker does not take all the talking time away from a newcomer. Or, you may want to mix the language levels so that the students can help each other. There is no right or wrong way to group students, and your groupings might look different every time.

Be explicit about what you would like the groups to accomplish. Clarify what their final product will look like. Provide an example or written directions when appropriate. Check to ensure that students understand what their task is before you send them off.

Figure 3.5
There is no right or wrong way to group children.

Let them know how they will get there. Tell the group what each member should do while they are working. Make sure you make your expectations clear. If it's not okay for one member of the group to sit back and watch quietly, make it known that you expect everyone to participate. Talk about problems that might come up and how to solve them. "What if you want to write something on the group's poster, but another group member has the pen?" Have the kids come up with the solutions so that when the problem comes up during their group time, they are well equipped to find a solution.

Monitor the group work, but don't hover authoritatively. Listen to what kids are saying and ask questions that show you are interested. Jump into conversations, but don't take over. This is the kids' time to talk and learn from each other. If something interesting comes up that you would like to talk about with the whole class, write it down so that you can bring it up later.

Address the problems that come up. Issues will arise, and it is important not to sweep them under the rug so that the work can continue. This does not help students learn to solve their own problems next time. Sometimes it is possible to talk with some students while the rest continue working. Other times, you might need to put everything on pause and call the students together for an impromptu class meeting. You may need to talk about what to do when you can't find a pencil, or it might be necessary to have a more serious conversation about what to do when someone in your group laughs at something you say. Either scenario is something that is bound to happen again. If you teach the students how to handle it next time, pretty soon group time will have few interruptions.

Allow groups to share their final products at the end of the work time. Let them do the talking and encourage other students to ask questions. Use reinforcing language to encourage active listening. For example, you might say, "Your question shows that you were really listening to the speaker," or "I was curious about that too! I'm glad you brought that up!"

Make time to reflect on how it was to work in a group. Ask the class what went well and what was hard. Help them brainstorm how they can make improvements the next time they work with a group. Sometimes this process seems tedious, but you'll see the payoff later when you notice that groups are working together well, kids are being kind to each other, and everyone is engaged whether you are close by or not.

10. Encourage Independence and Autonomy

The more things your students can do for themselves, the more time you have to do the important stuff—teach! You can help kids become independent, but it takes some work. The beginning of the year is a great time to start working on routines and procedures. Teach the kids how to follow a procedure, teach it again, model it, and practice it. Then observe as the kids follow through, and reinforce the things you see. Give them specific feedback about what you want them to do. The three Rs of teacher language (Brady, Forton, and Porter 2011) can help a teacher think about effective language to use when working with kids on routines and procedures. "Reinforcing" language acknowledges positive behaviors: "Timmy, I notice you are cleaning up your materials quickly!" "Reminding" language helps students remember and communicate their expectations before they start a task or at the first sign of inappropriate behavior: "What will you do after your group is excused?" or "Tell me again how you are supposed to handle the microscope." "Redirecting" language can be used when a student's behavior is clearly off track. "Stop shining the flashlight in Cindy's eye and shine it on the mirror instead." The "three Rs" help students learn and practice autonomy since they encourage the child to be accountable for his actions. This same language is great for managing transitions so that precious time needed for inquiry is not lost. After giving explicit directions for cleaning up, you might ask the students to remind you of what the expectations are and then reinforce and redirect as the students work.

Science time is filled with routines and procedures, and the more successful the kids are at independence, the more you can listen, take notes, and ask questions. Take time to teach kids your expectations and help them practice, so that these become second nature to them. My class recently worked in groups to create a battery out of a lemon and copper wire (see Chapter 6). Together, we read the directions given on the website, and I pointed out where to find all the materials. Then, I asked the students to choose their own groups and begin working. Although this could have been a recipe for disaster, the kids did a wonderful job since we had previously established the procedures for getting materials and starting to work quickly. The kids had practiced this many times before. Because of this, I was able to get right to work with a group of students.

It is also important for kids to be able to think and make decisions independently. And to learn how to do this, they need practice, and a lot of it. That means that you will want to give them as many opportunities to practice as they can. Give them choices whenever possible. Students might get to choose where they sit or with whom they want to work. You might let them have some choice in which assignments they are going to complete or the order in which they complete them. When you do give kids choices, be ready for them to make mistakes. Handle the mistakes like a learning opportunity and talk to them about how they can make better choices next time. Elementary students are just beginning to understand that the choices they make now can affect what happens down the road. So, if I choose to sit next to my best friend, I might be too silly and not be able to get my work done. It's important to allow kids to make these mistakes, as these are what will help them think about what is best the next time a choice awaits them. Similarly, expect successes and make sure you acknowledge them. When you notice that children have made wise choices, let them know you are proud of what they did and help them realize the positive effects of their actions. When kids are told what they are doing right, they are more likely to repeat these actions.

EFFECTIVE CLASSROOM MANAGEMENT: AN INVESTMENT THAT SAVES TIME

When you walk into Sharon's diverse classroom during inquiry science, you'll notice a buzz of activity as children engage in discussions about their theories, work together in groups on experiments, write in their science journals, and move about the room getting materials for projects. All of this activity requires that students know the rules and how to follow them. It requires that they know how to treat one another with respect, take turns, share materials, listen to one another's ideas, use materials carefully, and clean up after themselves. Inquiry science would not run smoothly if Sharon hadn't invested the time in helping her students learn to be independent and demonstrate self-control, or if she hadn't invited her students to share in the responsibility of creating the classroom rules so that they might feel a sense of ownership. Inquiry science works in Sharon's class because she explicitly teaches her students how to behave and provides time for them to practice these behaviors. It works because there is a morning meeting time at the beginning of each day when the class convenes on the rug to listen to each other's stories, solve problems, and learn how to care for one another. It works because Sharon uses the power of her words to respectfully reinforce students' appropriate behavior so that she has to do less reminding and redirecting.

I've heard many teachers complain that there just isn't time for morning meeting, or for taking the time during the first six weeks of school to teach students how to follow the classroom rules. It is no wonder that teachers feel this way; they are stressed out and buckling under the pressure of a high-stakes testing environment that places more value on the academic curriculum than on the social curriculum. Effective classroom management takes time, but it's time worth spending. In her book *Teaching Children to Care*, Ruth Charney wisely reminds us that "It is a challenge to help children grow up to be decent and kind, and to retain faith in ourselves, our children, our expectations. To meet these challenges, we need to know how to manage a classroom and how to teach our children to behave. We need to know how to pass on an affection for moral and ethical behavior in a difficult world" (2002, 12).

CHAPTER 4

SUPPORTING ENGLISH LANGUAGE LEARNERS IN THE DIVERSE CLASSROOM

Many factors contribute to a classroom's diversity. These include race, culture, ethnicity, socioeconomic status, learning styles, varied experiences and background knowledge, support from home, skill level, readiness, behavior, and students' proficiency level in English. Because they are among the fastest-growing demographic group of students in the United States, teaching English language learners has become a big challenge for teachers as they try to find ways to make content comprehensible and help students use English to communicate their understanding of the core content areas of mathematics, social studies, and science.

Just as diversity comes in many different forms in the classroom, English learners as a group are diverse as well. ELLs vary widely by level of schooling, parents' level of education, parents' proficiency in English, proficiency and literacy in their native language, and proficiency in English. Some English learners have had limited access to education, and some have experienced war firsthand or lived in refugee camps. Most ELLs are born in the United States, but the level of English spoken in their homes varies considerably (Wright 2010).

The students in Sharon's class are mostly English learners, but they are different from one another in many ways. For example, Diana is a student from Burma who is at the beginning level of English proficiency according to California's English Language Development Test (CELDT). She has had limited access to public education in her home country and struggles with academic content. Rafael was born in the United States, but his parents do not speak English. Although he is making good progress in school, his proficiency in English is at an intermediate level. Carlos is a gifted student whose English skills are advanced. His parents are bilingual and speak to him in both English and Spanish at home. These three students are examples of the range of experiences, backgrounds, and levels of proficiency that Sharon must consider when she plans and teaches her science lessons.

CHALLENGES LANGUAGE LEARNERS FACE DURING INQUIRY SCIENCE

When engaged in inquiry science, children must use language to make a prediction or a hypothesis. They use language when talking to a friend about how they'll set up an experiment. And they use language when they are reading about batteries, reflecting on the outcome of an investigation, writing about the conclusions they draw, or pondering new questions they have. Language can be a powerful learning tool during inquiry, promoting the understanding of science concepts (Rosebery, Warren, and Conant 1992). But when the language of instruction is unfamiliar to a student, English language learners can experience challenges that may create roadblocks to learning. These challenges are reflected in their scores on science achievement tests, which are well below that of their native English-speaking counterparts (Next Generation Science Standards Writing Team 2012).

English language learners face a triple challenge during science instruction. They must learn everyday vocabulary, content-specific vocabulary, and the language structures that are used when engaged in inquiry, such as formulating hypotheses, drawing conclusions, making inferences, and asking questions. The language of science can be confusing for English language learners because it uses many words from everyday life that have different meanings. For example, students may know that they eat off of a plate, but in science, plate tectonics has quite a different meaning. The same is true of the words *cell* (as in cell phone), *tissue* (something to use when you sneeze), and *organ* (an instrument). All of these words have meanings in everyday life that are different from the way they are used in science (Wright 2010). To create an equitable learning environment for English language learners during inquiry, teachers must be aware of their students' proficiency levels in English and determine the language demands of science lessons to plan for appropriate support during instruction. English language learners are entitled to high-quality language *and* content instruction so that they can use English to learn science and use science as a context for learning English. When we teach science, we are also teaching English, not just teaching *in* English.

DETERMINING THE ACADEMIC LANGUAGE DEMANDS OF A SCIENCE LESSON

When planning a science lesson, Sharon analyzes the language that students will be reading, writing, listening to, and having to produce. If students have to read from their science textbook or a piece of nonfiction, Sharon reads the text ahead of time, looking for any text features that might pose problems for her English learners. She asks herself many questions as she thinks about the language demands of the reading. Are there tricky definitions that might need to be discussed or recast in more accessible ways? Are there grammatical forms that might be challenging to readers, such as the conditional tense: *What might happen* if an earthquake occurs in a large city? Are there long, complex sentences that might need to be broken down into shorter sentences for the students? Are there idiomatic phrases that may be unfamiliar? Are there captions in the text that students might need to pay particular attention to? Are there transition words used (*unless, although, finally, because, consequently, therefore*), and will students need to learn what they indicate (Cloud, Genesee, and Hamayan 2009)?

Sharon also thinks about key vocabulary that her students might need to understand and use during inquiry. For example, when planning a unit on energy (see Chapter 6), Sharon determines what *everyday words* students will need to know and use (such as *rubber band, wire, flashlight, Styrofoam, paper, battery*) and what *content-specific vocabulary* they will need to learn (such as *electricity, conductor, energy, insulator*). As she thinks about when and how she will teach the terms, Sharon draws from a variety of strategies that make the vocabulary accessible and easier to learn. These include making use of realia or concrete materials to demonstrate usage (for example, using a real flashlight when introducing the word); creating an illustrated vocabulary chart to help students visualize the words; using familiar synonyms for academic terms (for example, *see-through* for *transparent*); and making students aware of cognates, which are words in English that sound similar in a student's native language (for example, the word *atomos* is Spanish for *atoms*). In addition to using these strategies to explicitly teach vocabulary, Sharon models using the words in context and has her students repeat them for practice.

The academic language that students must learn and use during inquiry science is not restricted to vocabulary. Students must also use the vocabulary in complete sentences to say something about their learning. So if a student is learning about minerals and wants to compare two different ones, she will need to know some describing words (*black, white, rough, smooth*) *and* be able to use them to compare the minerals (mineral A is white and smooth, whereas mineral B is black and rough). In other words, the student is using the vocabulary for a purpose: to compare minerals. In science, students use language during inquiry for a variety of purposes: to describe, compare, hypothesize, predict, sequence, categorize or classify, explain, analyze, draw conclusions, ask and answer questions, estimate, persuade, and identify.

Whenever we ask children to read something, say something, write something, or listen to our directions or a procedure during inquiry science, we are placing a language demand on them for which they may need extra support, depending upon their level of proficiency in English.

SETTING CONTENT AND LANGUAGE OBJECTIVES

When planning a science lesson, Sharon thinks about content and language as interconnected, because we use language to learn about science concepts, and we use science contexts to develop language. "Just as language (development) cannot occur if we only focus on subject matter, content knowledge cannot grow if we only focus on learning the English language" (Hill and Flynn 2006, 22).

When students use communication to make sense of the world, and when they talk or write about their learning, it gives the teacher a window into their thinking. Are their ideas correct? Do they hold naïve conceptions about a concept? Do their ideas hold merit? Language is an important learning tool and a key assessment tool. When Sharon thinks about the science content she will teach, she considers the language that students will use to show that they have learned the content. To help her provide the right support for students, she first sets a science-content objective (guided by the overall science standard or goal for the lesson), and then she thinks of a language objective that supports the content objective.

For example, for one of the lessons in a unit on energy, Sharon knew that students would be learning about different sources of energy (the science-content objective). She also knew that students would be thinking about, talking about, and then writing about what they think energy is. Because Sharon knew that her students would need to *describe* where energy comes from and what it is, she set a language objective: "Students will orally and in writing *describe* energy and where it comes from." Setting a language objective focuses Sharon's attention on the purpose for using language in a lesson (in this case, the purpose was *describing*). Setting a language objective also guides Sharon when she thinks about the support students will need when using language. In the lesson on energy, Sharon offered her students a simple writing prompt—*Energy is . . .*—to help them get started on their writing. The idea for the prompt flowed directly from the language objective.

In another lesson, on pendulums, Sharon's content objective was "Students will conduct multiple trials to test a prediction in a pendulum experiment." Her language objective, which supported the content objective, was "Students will *make predictions* about the pendulums orally and in writing." Writing a language objective helped Sharon focus on the purpose for using language in the lesson (making predictions), thereby helping her plan for linguistic support.

For a lesson on minerals, Sharon had to teach the following big idea or science standard over the course of a week: "Students know how to compare the physical properties of different kinds of rocks and know that a rock is composed of different combinations of minerals." The lesson she was going to teach that day from the rocks and minerals unit engaged students in performing tests. Sharon's content objective was "Students will perform a variety of tests to learn about the properties of minerals." Her language objective, which supported the content objective, was "Students will use key vocabulary to describe and compare the properties of minerals orally and in writing." The language objective for the lesson helped Sharon focus on what she wanted students to talk and write about during the lesson so that they would meet the content objective. It also helped guide her in creating the support students would need to describe and compare the minerals.

Native English speakers are able to perform the language functions of describing, predicting, and comparing when prompted with questions such as, Can you describe what energy is and where it comes from? What do you predict will happen when you perform the experiment with the pendulum? How does mineral A compare with mineral B? English language learners may understand the content of the lesson, but their inexperience with the language can keep them from articulating what they know. It is also possible that their struggles with the language of instruction lead them to partial or inaccurate understandings of the content. Until they verbalize their understandings, what they have learned or not learned remains a mystery to the teacher and may even be unclear to the students themselves. Choosing a language objective or language function that matches the science-content objective makes the learning more observable to the teacher and the student (Bresser, Melanese, and Sphar 2009).

Setting a content objective helps the teacher think about the science content she needs to focus on. Setting an accompanying language objective serves to highlight the language students will use during the lesson to indicate whether they are learning the science. Setting a language objective also guides the teacher in planning strategies that will support students when they communicate during inquiry.

PROVIDING SUPPORT

The support that we provide English language learners during inquiry science falls into three categories: strategies that make content comprehensible, strategies that provide opportunities for communication, and strategies that provide support for communication.

Making Content Comprehensible

The strategies that make science content comprehensible include ones that Sharon uses to help students access key vocabulary: the use of illustrated vocabulary banks, highlighting cognates, recasting science terms or using familiar synonyms, and providing realia and concrete materials. Sharon also uses gestures or acts out words, phrases, and directions when teaching.

She uses lots of visuals such as graphic organizers and pictures that help children "see" concepts. In addition, she modifies her teacher talk by slowing down and articulating clearly when giving directions, emphasizes key words, and avoids idiomatic phrases or slang. In addition to bridging new vocabulary with students' native languages, Sharon always taps their prior knowledge and experiences so that they can build on their current knowledge about science topics. All of these strategies help English language learners access science content because they allow them to visualize what the teacher is saying and connect what they are learning to what they already know.

Providing Opportunities for Communication

Sharon uses several different talk formats to provide students with the chance to discuss their learning. Whole-class discussions provide a forum in which there are many opportunities for the cross-pollination of ideas. Small-group formats create a safer environment in which more students get a chance to talk (see Figure 4.1). And partner talks give English language learners an even safer place to share ideas and rehearse what they might report in a whole-class setting. When partnering students during

Figure 4.1
Pair-shares provide a safe environment for English language learners.

pair-shares, Sharon sometimes places a student with advanced proficiency with a beginning-level English learner so that language modeling or translation can occur. At other times, she places two students together who are at the same proficiency level in English so that more talk can happen. Sharon might even let the students choose whom they want to pair-share with.

To begin a science discussion, Sharon might ask a question and then give students sufficient time (sometimes up to ten seconds) to gather their thoughts and generate a response before talking to the group or to their partner. Providing wait or think time is crucial for all students, but particularly for English language learners, who may need more time to think before sharing.

The use of wait time and the different talk formats provide opportunities for all English learners to think and then talk about their learning. But what if the students don't have the language (in English) to say something? This is when it is important for the teacher to offer structured support to assist students in communicating.

Providing Support for Communication

Sharon uses a variety of strategies to help her students communicate their science thinking and practice new words and phrases they are learning (see Figure 4.2). Some strategies are easy to use and take little time or effort. For example, Sharon might ask for a thumbs-up or thumbs-down after asking a question such as "Do you agree or disagree with Carlos's hypothesis?" Eliciting nonverbal responses supports English learners because the responses help teachers check for understanding without requiring students to produce language. English learners can participate and show that they understand a concept, or agree or disagree with someone's ideas, without having to talk. This is especially important for students whose comprehension of English is more advanced than their ability to speak the language.

Another easy strategy to use that supports students is having them give a choral response or echo in unison a new word or phrase. For example, when introducing the phrase *conductor of electricity*, Sharon had the class echo the phrase to her several times. This strategy exposes students to new vocabulary and serves as a model for correct pronunciation, syntax, and grammar. It also gives them practice using the language of science.

During a science lesson, students are exposed to many important concepts and ideas. These ideas may come from the teacher or from another

Makes Content Comprehensible	Provides Opportunities for Communication	Provides Support for Communication
Provide illustrated vocabulary banks Modify teacher talk Gesture/act out words, phrases, directions Highlight cognates Recast science terms Use concrete materials/realia Connect to prior learning Use graphic organizers	Use talk formats: • Partner talk • Table talk • Whole-group discussion Use wait time	Elicit nonverbal responses Elicit choral responses Have students repeat or reword Use sentence frames/prompts Differentiate questions

Figure 4.2 • Strategies, Activities, and Tools to Support English Learners

student in the class. One strategy that holds students responsible for listening is having them repeat or reword someone else's idea. Although repeating may not seem like a high-level task, it is much more active than simply listening to the concepts as they are presented. Rewording encourages students to express a new concept in their own language, a language we know they understand. Students can repeat or reword statements made by the teacher or by other students. The teacher can also repeat or reword statements made by students to emphasize or question information (Bresser, Melanese, and Sphar 2009).

Sentence Frames and Prompts

Two effective tools that help students say something about their learning are sentence frames and prompts. Prompts can be oral or written and are used as sentence starters. For example, during an inquiry lesson on energy, Sharon showed the class a video and then had them talk and write about what they learned. She provided the following prompts to jump-start their thinking and writing:

> *I learned . . .*
> *I wonder . . .*

In another lesson on UV beads, Sharon provided the following prompts to help students formulate testable questions:

What if . . . ?
Does . . . ?
I wonder . . . ?
What will happen if . . . ?
Is it possible to _____ ?

Sentence frames serve a variety of purposes. They provide the support English language learners need to fully participate in science discussions, serve to contextualize and bring meaning to vocabulary, provide a structure for practicing and extending English language skills, and help students use the vocabulary they learn in grammatically correct, complete sentences (Bresser, Melanese, and Sphar 2009).

During a unit on energy, Sharon wanted the students to make a prediction about a pair of students' hypothesis. To help them make a prediction, she provided the following frames. The first frame is appropriate for beginning-level English learners. Sharon differentiated the second frame for intermediate/advanced English learners. Notice how the second frame includes the conjunction *because*. This prompts the learners to explain their thinking further but requires more language:

I predict _____ hypothesis will work/won't work.
I predict _____ hypothesis will work/won't work because _____ .

During an investigation of UV beads, Sharon offered the following frame to help students describe the beads:

The beads are _____ and made of _____ .

To create sentence frames, Sharon first thinks about what key vocabulary students will need to know and understand. She then thinks about the purpose for using language. Will students be using vocabulary to make predictions about a hypothesis? Draw conclusions about an experiment? Compare minerals? Describe an energy source? Ask questions about UV beads? Explain how they got a toy car to move? Sharon tries to anticipate what students will say, and this guides her in creating the frames. When structured appropriately, sentence frames are flexible enough to be useful in a variety of contexts and open enough to allow students to give us their own ideas. These frames allow students to use the key vocabulary terms and put together complete thoughts, thoughts that can be connected, confirmed, rejected, revised, and understood. What's important is that the teacher model using the frames and give students practice so that they will actually use the frames during instruction.

The chart in Figure 4.3 includes examples of sentence frames for different topics in science and for different language functions or purposes for using language. The examples also include frames that are differentiated for different levels of English proficiency: beginning and intermediate/advanced.

Supporting Students at Different Proficiency Levels

As mentioned, the students in Sharon's class represent a wide range of proficiency levels in English. For example, John and Felicia are native English

Language Function	Science Topic	Beginning Level	Intermediate/Advanced Levels
Describing	Animal Structures	The mealworm has/is ___. **Example:** The mealworm has <u>six legs</u>.	The mealworm has/is ___, ___, and ___. **Example:** The mealworm has <u>a head</u>, <u>antennae</u>, and <u>six legs</u>.
Comparing	Rocks and Minerals	Mineral ___ is ___, and mineral ___ is ___. **Example:** Mineral <u>B</u> is <u>white</u>, and mineral <u>F</u> is <u>gray</u>.	Mineral ___ is ___, whereas mineral ___ is ___. Both are/have ___. **Example:** Mineral <u>B</u> is <u>white</u>, whereas mineral <u>F</u> is <u>gray</u>. Both are <u>opaque</u>.
Predicting	Pendulums	I predict that the ___ will ___. **Example:** I predict that the <u>number of cycles</u> will <u>be about 15</u>.	I predict that the ___ will ___, because ___. **Example:** I predict that the <u>number of cycles</u> will <u>be about 15</u>, because <u>when we swung the pendulum before, one cycle took 2 seconds</u>.
Describing Cause and Effect	Liquids and Solids	NA	If ___, then ___. **Example:** If <u>I mix vinegar with baking soda</u>, then <u>the solid and liquid combined fizzes and creates a gas</u>. *(continued)*

Figure 4.3 • Language Functions and Sentence Frames Chart

Sequencing	Experimentation	First _____. Next _____. Finally, _____. **Example:** First I made a guess. Next, I put the oil and soap on the beads. Finally, I put them outside to see what would happen.	First _____. Next _____. Then _____. After that, _____. Finally, _____. **Example:** First I made a hypothesis. Next I put the oil and soap on the beads. Then I put the beads outside. After that, I observed the beads to see what would happen. Finally, I recorded the results of the experiment.
Hypothesizing	Energy	If ___, then ___. **Example:** If you put metal between the wires and the batteries, then the bulb will light.	If ___, then ___, because ___. **Example:** If you put metal between the wires and the batteries, then the bulb will light, because I think the metal conducts electricity.
Asking Questions	Any Topic	Beginners may need additional support with asking questions.	What if . . . ? Does . . . ? I wonder . . . . What will happen if . . . ? When comparing ___ and ___, which will . . . ? Is it possible to . . . ?
Categorizing	Animals	These ___, and these ___. **Example:** These have fur, and these don't have fur.	These ___, and these ___. Therefore, these ___ and these ___. **Example:** These animals have fur, and these animals don't have fur. Therefore, these are mammals and these are not mammals.
Drawing Conclusions	Ultraviolet Rays	NA	When I ___, ___. Therefore, I conclude that ___. **Example:** When I put sunscreen on the beads, they didn't change color in the sun. Therefore, I conclude that the sunscreen blocks UV rays.
Identifying/ Explaining	Atoms and Molecules	This is a/an ___. **Example:** This is an atom.	This is a/an ___. I know this because ___. **Example:** This is an atom. I know this because it has a nucleus, protons, and electrons.

Figure 4.3 • Language Functions and Sentence Frames Chart *(continued)*

speakers who require little linguistic support during inquiry science, although sentence frames for advanced proficiency levels can push them to use more sophisticated language.

Carlos and Benito are at advanced and intermediate levels of English proficiency, respectively, and with some added grammatical support, are able to perform all of the language functions that John and Felicia can. For example, when Carlos makes a grammatical error, Sharon models correct usage and has him repeat it to her. These two students, like everyone in Sharon's class, also need exposure to and support for using academic terms during inquiry science. They also need practice talking like scientists, since the language they are expected to use during inquiry is more formal than the English they use on the playground.

Students who are native English speakers, and those who are at advanced and intermediate levels of English proficiency, are able to respond to more open-ended questions during inquiry. For example, Sharon might ask, "What do you think will happen when we use the lemon to make a battery?" This is a good question for native English speakers and those at advanced and intermediate levels of proficiency. But a response to this question requires a lot of language for beginning-level English learners. These students must produce so much language just to structure their answer that they might choose not to answer at all.

Jackie, Alejandra, and Dao are at the beginning stages of English language development and need lots of visual support. They understand more English than they can produce, and the questions that Sharon asks them are sometimes different from the questions she poses to students at more advanced levels. For example, to improve his participation, Sharon might ask Dao a question that requires a nonverbal or one-word response. (For example, "Do you agree with Carlos's hypothesis?" or "Thumbs-up if you agree with Carlos's hypothesis.") Sharon might ask Dao a question that requires only a physical response. ("Point to the materials that make the bulb light up" or "Can you show me how to make the bulb light up?") Sometimes Sharon will build the answer into the question. ("Which works better, the potato or the lemon?")

Figure 4.4 shows what students at different levels of English proficiency can do, what support they need, and the types of questions that are most effective to ask.

When thinking about support for students at different proficiency levels, it's important to hold high expectations for all students. Just because a student is beginning to learn English doesn't mean he isn't good at science! And just because a student at the beginning stages of English language

Level	What They Can Do	Support They Need	Types of Questions to Ask
Beginning	One-word or nonverbal responses, can identify, match, categorize, and produce simple sentences	Lots of visual and manipulative support	Questions that elicit one-word, nonverbal, or physical responses, build the answer into the question
Intermediate/ Advanced	Can describe, explain, define, retell, compare and contrast, justify, and more	Grammatical support	More open-ended questions, questions that model the structure of an answer

Figure 4.4 • Support for Different Proficiency Levels in English

development typically struggles with responding to open-ended questions doesn't mean we can't ask them. When Sharon asks an open-ended question, she first asks everyone to think about it. If individual students need a more structured or modified form of the question in order to respond, she will provide one. Sharon's goal is for *everyone* to improve and move forward in their English language development, and she uses inquiry science as a context for them to do so.

EQUITABLE ACCESS FOR ALL STUDENTS

During inquiry science, Sharon wants all of her students to have access to science content. If language is a barrier to learning, she provides the necessary support. Without support, many of her students might not be able to participate in science discussions or express their learning through the language of instruction. Providing explicit language support is critical to equitable access. Lisa Delpit frames this idea in her book *Other People's Children* (1999). She urges educators to explicitly teach those forms of language that will enable students to succeed in school and actively participate in their learning communities. Therefore, when we expect the students in our diverse classrooms to contribute their ideas during science discussions, we need to make sure that they have the skills in English to do so.

CHAPTER 5

DIVING INTO INQUIRY: INVESTIGATING UV BEADS

Teachers are often hesitant to teach science because they think they have to know everything about the world and how it works. But this is far from the truth. Although content knowledge is important to teaching science, teachers don't have to be experts. Even biologists don't necessarily know everything about rocks and minerals, and chemists aren't always the best people to go to if you have a question about insects! But pedagogical content knowledge, or the ability to make ideas accessible to others, is important. And engaging students in the inquiry process by asking good questions and offering interesting experiences that prompt children to ask good questions is also critical.

Most important to being a good science teacher is holding the expectation that *all* children can be scientists and think critically. Providing a thinking curriculum is especially important for those children in diverse classrooms who have been underserved by our educational system. Lisa

Delpit, in *Multiplication Is for White People*, bemoans the state of the "pedagogy of poverty" by observing that "The reductionism that is proliferating in classrooms where low-income children of color spend their days is alarming. In the name of 'test prep,' students spend hours and hours completing worksheets that are presumably meant to increase their test scores on standardized tests" (2012, 123). The teaching and learning discussed in this chapter reveals a promising alternative to the sort of reductionism to which Delpit is referring.

Investigating UV-detecting beads is a science activity that is simple, open ended, and will help teachers feel comfortable teaching from an inquiry perspective *and* hook students on the excitement of science. We got the idea from Charles R. Pearce's book, *Nurturing Inquiry: Real Science for the Elementary Classroom* (1999). As the students investigate the UV beads, they learn to ask questions, develop hypotheses, describe the steps in their experiments, analyze the results, draw conclusions, and then move beyond their conclusions by asking new questions. And as the students dive into inquiry, Sharon supports them in a variety of ways.

Sharon prepares for the lesson by ordering UV-detecting beads from Educational Innovations (5 Francis J. Clarke Circle, Bethel, CT 06801; for phone orders, [888] 912-7474). She plans her lessons so that students will have the opportunity to identify and distinguish between research and testable science questions, and engage in the inquiry cycle. She also plans to make sure that students will have the linguistic support necessary to use the language functions of describing, asking questions, hypothesizing, sequencing the steps to experiments, and reporting results. She thinks ahead about how to help her diverse group of students manage materials and manage their behavior during inquiry science. And Sharon familiarizes herself with the science of ultraviolet rays, which are invisible rays that are part of the energy that comes from the sun. She learns about UV rays by engaging in the inquiry cycle: she thinks about what she already knows, asks questions about what she wants to know, and then searches for the answers to her questions from friends, scientists, and even the Internet. This inquiry process strengthens Sharon's content knowledge and helps her think of questions to ask her students during the lessons.

DAY 1

Making and Describing Bead Bracelets

Sharon begins the investigation by calling Tina Rasori's thirty-one fifth graders to the front rug. Sharon is the guest teacher for this three-day lesson sequence, and several of the children are her former students and greet her with wide smiles.

"Today we're going to begin a three-day investigation," Sharon says. She holds up a plastic bag full of white beads and continues, "We'll start our lesson by using string and some of these white beads to make a bracelet. Then we'll take the bracelets outside and see what happens to them." Sharon has two volunteers distribute three beads and a piece of string to each student. She tells them to make a bracelet and describe the beads to someone next to them (see Figure 5.1).

Soon there's a lot of chatter, and Sharon uses reinforcing language to encourage students to describe their beads, saying, "I'm noticing that people are helping one another make the bracelets, and I'm beginning to hear a lot of partners describe their beads." Focusing on what students *should* be doing or saying helps prevent her from having to remind or redirect students during inquiry science.

Figure 5.1
UV bead
bracelets

As Sharon listens in, she notices that some students are already starting to make predictions. A few wonder what will happen when they take the beads outside and whether the beads will change in some way.

After a minute or so, Sharon calls for the students' attention and elicits their descriptions: slippery, plastic, round, small, decorative, white. Sharon encourages the children to use complete sentences (for example, "The beads are white and made of plastic") when describing the beads, and at times she models complete sentences for the English learners who are at the beginning stages of proficiency. Sentence frames are also useful in helping English learners frame descriptions: *The beads are _____ and made of _____.*

Taking the Bracelets Outside

Before taking the class outside, Sharon asks the students to think and talk about appropriate behavior on the playground, because recess is over and other classes will be engaged in learning. The students then line up and walk outside with their bead bracelets. Almost instantly, the students' beads begin to change color from white to shades of purple, pink, yellow, and blue. There are lots of oohs and ahhs, and everyone is excited, commenting on their beads (see Figures 5.2 and 5.3). Sharon urges them on by asking, "What are you noticing? Talk with the people around you."

Figure 5.2
Observing the
UV beads
change colors

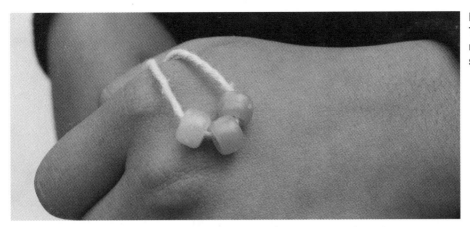

Figure 5.3
The UV beads
responding to
sunlight

"It's like a pattern: blue, red, blue."

"Oh my gosh! They're changing!"

"I wonder if it's activated by heat."

"What's inside that makes them change color?"

"In the dark they're white, but in the sun they change colors!"

Everyone is engaged, making observations, and asking questions. After about five minutes, Sharon gathers the students and leads them back into the classroom to talk more about what they've observed.

Brainstorming About the Beads

When the students enter the room, the level of excitement is still very high; everyone is chatting about the beads. Rather than working against this enthusiasm, Sharon has the students sit on the rug and talk in groups about what they're noticing. After a minute or so, she calls the class to attention and they begin to brainstorm.

"They're getting lighter!" Juan exclaims.

"My heat theory is coming true!" Eduardo says, grinning from ear to ear.

"What do you mean?" Sharon asks.

Eduardo explains that when he was outside, he theorized that heat activates the beads to make them change color, and since it's cooler in the classroom, the beads are changing back to white.

Melinda agrees with Eduardo and says, "It turned white because outside it's warm and inside it's not."

"So you both think that heat causes the beads to change?" Sharon asks, summarizing the students' comments.

Mario disagrees. "I think if the light shines on the bead, then it changes color."

"Where does the light come from?" Sharon probes.

"The sun!" several students respond.

"The sun turns the beads different colors; they're like glow sticks that have chemicals inside," Guillermo says, making a connection to his prior experience.

"No—in the hallway they changed too," Linda counters.

Amanda adds, "But outside it was brightest, and the beads changed color more."

These kinds of arguments are what Sharon hopes for during inquiry science, and they most often occur when she talks less and listens more. Sharon has learned to value the knowledge and experiences that children bring to the classroom.

Identifying Research and Testable Questions

"Okay, we've talked about what you noticed about the beads; now I want you to think of some questions you have about them," Sharon says. She gives the students a few seconds of individual think time and then charts their questions on the board. She provides the following prompts to help all the students, but especially the English language learners in the class, frame questions:

> *What if . . .?*
> *Does . . .?*
> *I wonder . . . .*
> *What will happen if . . .?*
> *When comparing _____ with _____, which will _____?*
> *Is it possible to _____?*

Following are some of the students' questions:

If we turned on the lights, then would the beads change color?
I think we should put them in the water and see if they change colors.
Does oil make them change color?
Why do the beads change color?
Does soap make them change color?
What will happen if we put sunscreen on the beads?
Does motion make them change color?

I wonder what is inside the beads.

What would happen if we heat them up inside?

What are the beads made out of?

When comparing different types of sunscreen, which will keep the beads from changing color?

Is it possible to keep the beads from changing color?

After writing all their questions on the board, Sharon asks the students to think about which ones can be tested in an experiment and which ones need to be researched, either by reading about it or asking an expert. As they identify testable and research questions, Sharon writes an *R* for "research" and a *T* for "testable" next to each question. For example, Why do the beads change color? is a research question, and What will happen if we put sunscreen on the beads? is a testable question.

To finish the first day's lesson, Sharon gives each student a piece of paper and directs them to write down a testable question they are interested in and a list of the materials they would need to perform an experiment to answer their question. To make sure students don't lose their bead bracelets, Sharon gives them each a piece of masking tape with which to attach their bracelet to their desktop. When students are finished writing, she collects their papers.

DAY 2

Having a Tea Party

The class assembles on the rug for Day 2 of the investigation, and Sharon tells them they're going to have a tea party. Several students ask what a tea party is, and Sharon explains that during a tea party, people mingle and move from person to person, talking and drinking tea. "In today's tea party, there won't be any tea, but I want you to share the question you wrote down yesterday about the beads."

As Amanda distributes the papers from yesterday, Kyle grabs his paper from her. Kyle is a bright but challenging student who has a quick temper and often tests the limits. Sharon notices this and immediately addresses the situation. "Papers are not for grabbing," she says in a firm and commanding voice, focusing her words on Kyle's actions. Kyle laughs, and says that Amanda wouldn't give him his paper. "Kyle, would you want me to grab my paper from you like that?" She doesn't get a response from him, so

Sharon continues, "You owe Amanda an apology, *right now*." Reluctantly, Kyle apologizes.

Although Sharon risked getting into a power struggle with Kyle, she wanted to demonstrate to the class that respecting others is important during inquiry science. And she wanted to communicate to Kyle that she holds high expectations for him. During inquiry, one of Sharon's management goals is to take care of the little things before they escalate and become big problems during a lesson. Rather than using rewards to motivate students to follow directions and get along with others, Sharon relies on her strong personal connections with students. She is direct and firm with them when necessary, but she also lets them know when they are doing the right thing by using positive, reinforcing language. Sharon spends time explicitly teaching students how to communicate respectfully during morning meeting. And she follows up on problem situations using social conferences, during which she checks in with students about conflicts that arise in the classroom. In these conferences, Sharon explores with individual children the reasons behind their behaviors and identifies possible solutions. The goal is to set behavioral boundaries and involve the child in the problem-solving process.

Once everyone has their papers, Sharon tells the class to mingle and share their inquiry question with at least five different people. The tea party gets the students up and walking around, and it provides a context for reading their inquiry questions. After a few minutes, Sharon counts down from ten to zero and directs the class to reassemble on the rug. Once they are settled, she asks each student to make eye contact with a person whose inquiry question is of interest to them, and then to sit next to that person. Sharon sees that Kyle quickly and quietly finds his partner, Melinda; Sharon whispers to him that she notices this and appreciates that he's following directions.

Providing Support for Writing

Once everyone has a partner, Sharon models how to write a hypothesis. She first asks the class if they know what one is, and several students say it's like a prediction. Then she writes the following sentence frame on the board:

If _____, *then* _____.

Sentence frames help all students, but especially English language learners, use the language of science to talk or write about their learning during a science experiment or a discussion. To ensure that students will actually use the frame, Sharon models using it aloud with an example, and then has the class echo: "If <u>I put red paint on the beads</u>, then <u>they won't change colors</u>."

"After you write your hypothesis, you and your partner will ask an adult in the room for the materials you need for your experiment that will answer your inquiry question," Sharon tells the class. She points to a table in the back of the room where she's placed a variety of materials the students had requested for their experiments: different types of sunscreen, bowls for hot and cold water, vegetable oil, liquid soap, and a portable heater.

"Once you do your experiment, you'll need to write up the procedure and the results," Sharon continues. She then writes on the board the following sentence starters, ones that focus on sequencing the events in an experiment, and has the students practice reading them aloud:

First _____.
Next, _____.
Then, _____.
After that, _____.
Finally, _____.
Results: _____.

The Home-School Connection

As Sharon circulates around the room and monitors students' progress, the student teacher and a parent volunteer work at the materials table helping the children get what they need. Materials management can be tricky during inquiry science, and placing everything in a central location with an adult handing out materials makes things run smoothly. Bringing in volunteers to help is a challenge, because many of the students' parents are busy all day at their jobs or dealing with the many problems that come with living in poverty.

Although it is sometimes difficult for families to schedule time to visit the classroom, inquiry science is a perfect time to invite them to school and participate. Sharon values what Dr. Luis Moll (Moll et al. 1992) refers to as families' *funds of knowledge*. These are the skills, strategies, and wisdom generated by groups of people, but they are sometimes overlooked by educators. Reaching out to families, finding out what they have to offer the classroom, and making them feel appreciated is especially important for groups who have been undervalued by society.

Sharon is proactive in her efforts to communicate with families. She meets with each family at the beginning of the school year to build a relationship and to determine the funds of knowledge that parents can offer the classroom. She writes letters informing families about what's going on during science time, inviting them to the classroom to help out. Sharon elicits help from the school, the district office, or someone in the community to translate the letters into the many native languages spoken at her school. She takes time to touch base with parents when they pick up their children at the end of the day, encouraging them to visit on the school's "Family Friday," a routine that the principal started to encourage family participation. And Sharon allows parents to bring younger siblings so that child care isn't a barrier to participation. If necessary, home visits can be a helpful way to reach out to families who feel that the school culture is intimidating and foreign. On these home visits, a teacher can share ideas about how to make science connections in the kitchen, at mealtimes, and outdoors. The teacher can also suggest that parents ask their children questions such as, Which solids turn to liquids? How fast does it take an ice cube to melt? How long does it take to boil water? What happens when you mix baking soda with vinegar? Can you describe the trees and plants in our backyard? What is the shape of the moon? What do you predict the moon will look like tomorrow night? Do you notice a pattern? Teachers can encourage parents to ask all sorts of science questions, and they can emphasize that it is important that children ask their own questions.

Experimenting with UV Beads

As the students settle into their chairs, they begin chatting about how to set up their experiments, how to write their hypotheses, and which materials they'll need for their investigations. Sharon makes a point to first check in with Kyle, the boy she disciplined during the first part of the lesson.

"It seems like you're in a bad mood—is that right, Kyle?" Sharon asks. Kyle nods. "Is there anything I can help you with so that you can get through the morning successfully?" Kyle doesn't seem ready to talk about what is bothering him, but at least Sharon gives him the opportunity to do so. She finds that social conferences give her a chance to find out what's behind students' actions, because she knows that children behave the way they do for a reason. Sometimes a child who acts out just needs some positive attention, and once Sharon shows Kyle that she is truly interested in his feelings, his behavior improves dramatically.

At first, it is quite chaotic in the room. Partners are trying to figure out how they'll conduct their experiments, students are lining up to get materials, hands are raised to get help from Sharon, and the noise level is definitely above a healthy buzz. Wouldn't it be easier just to have everyone investigate the same inquiry question? This is a question Sharon has asked herself before, but she has learned to be patient through the initial chaos because she knows that letting the students pursue their own questions will pay off in the long run. And she's right. The longer they work, the more the students settle down and focus; soon, everyone is busy experimenting. Letting them pursue their own questions gives the students a real stake in the results, and it honors their curiosity and their ideas.

Nang and his partner are applying sunscreen to some of their beads and are ready to take them outside to see if they change color. Michelle and Latesha use two different types of sunscreen and are comparing them to see which one is more effective. Kenneth is carrying a bowl of water outside to see if the beads change color once they are submerged. Kyle puts vegetable oil on some beads and dish soap on others and places them on the pathway just outside the room. Kenneth comes back into the room and asks Sharon if he should compare hot water and cold water, and Sharon replies, "I don't know—you're the scientist!"

The students seem to have an innate sense of how to conduct experiments, and their engagement is impressive. One question leads to another, and the students' voices are humming with the sound of scientists at work!

Pushing Students Beyond Their Initial Conclusions

As the students busy themselves with their experiments, Sharon sits down with Luis and Cesar, who are talking about what they discovered about oil (see Figure 5.4).

Luis: Oil makes the beads change quicker.

Cesar: Yeah, the sun helped the oil.

Sharon: What do you mean?

Cesar: The oil is hot and the sun is hot, so they changed faster.

Sharon: So is it the sun that helped the oil or the oil that helped the sun?

Cesar: Maybe we could have a race! We could put some in oil and some not and then put them in the sun. We can see which one changes first!

Figure 5.4
Cesar and Luis
talk about their
experiment.

The boys gather their materials and go outside to see what will happen. Sharon is pleased that her questions have helped the boys move beyond their initial conclusion: that the oil is hot and helps the sun change the color of the beads. Helping children confront their initial conceptions by asking questions and providing experiences that can help them move forward in the inquiry process is an important part of the teacher's role in inquiry science.

After a few minutes, Cesar and Luis run back into the room to report what they've discovered. They are huffing and puffing and excited to share. These boys are usually a handful in the classroom, but inquiry science has harnessed their energy, and they now have ownership of their learning.

> **Cesar:** The sun changes the color! The beads didn't change in the oil!
> **Luis:** Yeah, the sun produces energy, and energy changes the color.
> **Sharon:** What is this energy that the sun produces?
> **Luis and Cesar:** Computers and flowers use energy. The energy is from the sun.
> **Luis:** Energy flows to us. It's like electricity.
> **Sharon:** So the sun has electricity?
> **Cesar:** It's like fire!

Sharon: How is the sun like fire?

Cesar: They are both light and hot.

Sharon: Would the beads change if they were in front of a fire?

Cesar: No. It needs solar.

Excited, Cesar now wants to pursue a new question: Will the beads change color in front of a fire or a heater? Sharon is pleased that the boys are continuing the inquiry cycle by asking new questions and testing them out on their own.

Summarizing Discoveries

Cleanup is quite a production, and Sharon is careful to make sure everyone hears her directions. Students finish writing up the procedure and results of their experiments, put their materials away on the back table, and secure their bead bracelets on their desktops with masking tape. Finally, everyone is assembled at the front rug area.

Sharon leads a discussion that focuses mainly on sunscreen and what happened when it was applied to the beads and the beads were put in the sun. Amanda reports that the beads still changed color, "but at a slower rate." Melinda says that her beads "changed color completely, even with the sunscreen on" (Figure 5.5). Several students disagree and theorize that sunscreen is beneficial because "it slows down the damage that the sun can do to your skin." Sharon tells the class that she spends hundreds of dollars on sunscreen every year. "Do you think it's worth it?" she asks.

"Yes!" the students respond in unison.

Sharon thinks that discussing science beyond the end of an experiment is important, because she's noticed that many times, the scientific process in elementary school stops at the conclusion. When she visits the fifth-grade science fair, for example, she always asks the kids, "Why do you think that happened that way?" and they look at her like she's an alien. Kids don't often engage in the

Figure 5.5 Melinda discovered that her beads changed color even with sunscreen on them.

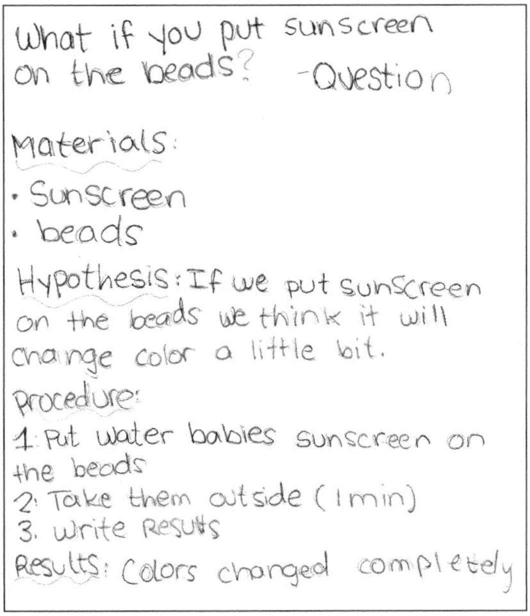

What if you put sunscreen on the beads? -Question

Materials:
· Sunscreen
· beads

Hypothesis: If we put sunscreen on the beads we think it will change color a little bit.

Procedure:
1. Put water babies sunscreen on the beads
2. Take them outside (1 min)
3. Write Results

Results: Colors changed completely

process of asking questions *after* they make a discovery. This is the process that Sharon thinks is most important during science. She thinks that encouraging children to wonder beyond the conclusion of a science experiment can help turn "cookbook" science into inquiry science.

DAY 3

Sharing Discoveries in Small Groups

Sharon begins the third and final day of the investigation by giving the students about fifteen minutes at their seats to finish writing the procedure and the results of their experiments. Then she has the students bring their papers to the rug and sit with their partners.

"Today we're going to share our experiments with each other," Sharon says. "First we'll have one partnership share with another." Sharon likes to provide different formats for discussion in her classroom: whole-class discussions, small-group discussions, and partner talks. These formats serve different purposes. Whole-class discussions allow for a broad cross-pollination of ideas. During small-group discussions, students still have the opportunity to share a variety of ideas, but in a safer environment. And during partner talks, students have even more opportunities to talk in a context where they can safely share their ideas. Partner talks are especially effective for English learners who need practice rehearsing before reporting their ideas to the whole class.

Before they begin, Sharon calls up two partnerships and has them model in front of the class. As they share, she highlights the protocol that she wants the students to follow: listen, take turns, be respectful, ask clarifying questions, and make connections. Sharon doesn't take for granted that the students have internalized how to share with one another.

As the students begin their presentations, Sharon realizes that although she has modeled the protocol, she still has to work hard to manage a few students during the partnership sharing. Some of the behaviors she observes are typical of those demonstrated by students who have not learned how to participate in conversations during inquiry science.

Sharon notices that Sovann, a student with a very troubled life, frequently interrupts his partner. He wants to share his ideas without waiting and listening. He is silly and disrespectful. Sharon gently pulls Sovann aside; she doesn't want to conference with him in front of his peers, because this might set him off, causing him embarrassment. When they are alone and away from the group, Sharon tells him what she's noticing, and then firmly gives him a choice: follow the protocol, or find some independent work and join the group when he feels he is ready. Sometimes a brief "time-out" away from the class can help a student regain his self-control and prepare him to come back to learning with the group.

Discussions during inquiry science do not always go smoothly, and Sharon is not a perfect teacher who walks into a classroom and magically makes the kids love science so much that their behavior is perfect. She works hard throughout the year, especially during morning meeting, to model the behaviors she expects, and she provides many opportunities for students to practice listening and sharing to build the skills necessary to participate during inquiry science.

Sharing Discoveries with the Class

After about five minutes of small-group sharing, Sharon calls the class back to attention and asks for volunteers to report what happened during their experiments, or to share any ideas they now have about why the beads changed color.

Andie starts the conversation by saying that he thinks it was the heat of the sun that changed the beads. Several people immediately jump in and respectfully disagree. Sharon notices, and uses reinforcing language by giving them positive feedback about how they "respectfully argued with one another, just like scientists do."

Arnie goes next. He's a newcomer who speaks Karen, one of the languages spoken in his native Thailand. Arnie has been listening intently to the conversation and tentatively raises his hand to contribute. When Sharon calls on him, the class quietly listens as Arnie disagrees with Andie by saying, "Because there is something special about the sun's light that makes the beads change color." This statement lights up the faces of many students in the room, and several relate anecdotes that seem to support Arnie's idea.

Michelle and Monica go next and read from their paper (Figure 5.6). They tell the class that they wondered what would happen if you put some of the beads in the shade and some in the sun. They share their discovery that both groups changed colors. Daniel asks the girls why they thought the beads would change color in the shade. They respond by explaining that "the light still gets to the beads in the shade, but not as much."

Sharon is pleased that the students are breaking out of the typical discourse pattern of teacher-student-teacher. One of her goals for students is

Figure 5.6
Michelle and
Monica
wondered what
would happen if
you put some
beads in the
sun and some
in the shade.

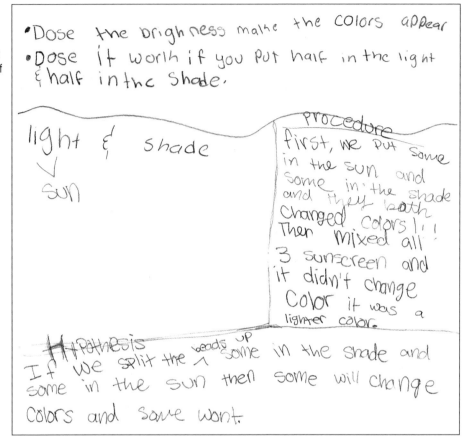

• Dose the brighness make the colors appear
• Dose it worth if you put half in the light
  & half in the Shade.

light & shade
  ↓
 sun

Procedure
first, we put some
in the sun and
some in the shade
and they both
Changed colors !!!
Then mixed all
3 sunscreen and
it didn't change
Color it was a
lighter color.

Hypothesis
If we split the beads up some in the shade and
some in the sun then some will change
colors and some wont.

to have them ask each other questions rather than having every interaction mediated by the teacher. She wants the students to feel empowered and develop the notion that not all of the knowledge flows from the teacher.

Finally, Kyle shares that when he put oil and soap on the beads and took them outside, they turned brighter colors, and that it took only one minute for the beads to change color in the sun (Figure 5.7).

Sharon closes the discussion by summarizing what many of the students discovered: that the beads changed color because of the sun's light. She then asks the class if they have heard of UV before. Several students make connections to commercials on television or having read about UV on sunscreen bottles. Sharon reveals to the class that the beads she provided were ultraviolet-detecting beads, and briefly explains to the students that UV rays "are invisible rays that are part of the energy that comes from the sun."

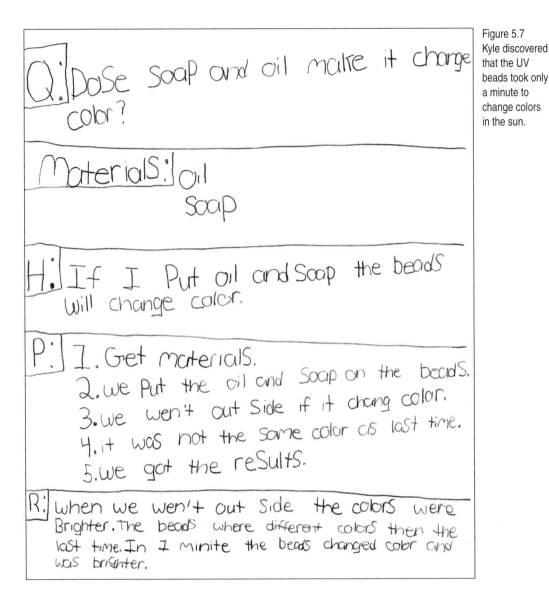

Q: Dose soap and oil make it change color?

Materials: oil
Soap

H: If I Put oil and Soap the beads will change color.

P: 1. Get materials.
2. we Put the oil and Soap on the beads.
3. we wen't out Side if it chang color.
4. it was not the Same color as last time.
5. we got the results.

R: when we wen't out Side the colors were Brighter. The beads where different colors then the last time. In 1 minite the beads changed color and was brighter.

Figure 5.7
Kyle discovered that the UV beads took only a minute to change colors in the sun.

Will this information lead to a research project on ultraviolet rays? Perhaps. But isn't that what inquiry science is all about: starting with questions about how the world works, and then ending with new ones?

CHAPTER 6

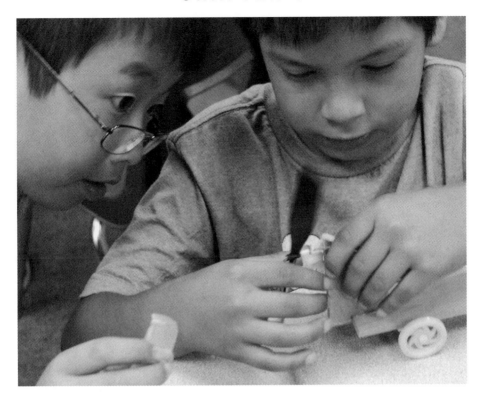

WHAT MAKES TOY CARS MOVE? A UNIT ON ENERGY

In his article in *Phi Delta Kappan*, educator Martin Haberman lists twelve ways to promote real learning rather than replicate a "pedagogy of poverty" (1991). The lessons in this chapter exemplify several of Haberman's recommendations: helping children see major concepts rather than isolated facts; involving children in planning what they will be doing; actively involving students in heterogeneous groups; directly involving students in real-life experiences; asking students to think about ideas that question common sense; and involving students in reflecting on their own lives.

The Scientific and Engineering Practices articulated in the Next Generation Science Standards (Next Generation Science Standards Writing Team 2012) help facilitate Haberman's recommendations. As you'll see, students in these lessons are actively engaged in asking questions, developing and using models, planning and carrying out investigations, constructing explanations, engaging in argument from evidence, and obtaining and communicating information.

DAY 1

Launching the Energy Unit

Sharon launches the unit on energy by asking a question: What makes toy cars move? Her fourth graders are gathered on the rug, and after several seconds of think time, Sharon facilitates a discussion. She uses the Socratic method—that is, teaching by asking questions rather than telling. Her goal is for students to construct their own understanding of how the world works through experimentation and discussion. This type of instruction, one that focuses on critical thinking, is not common for schools in low-income neighborhoods. Students of color and those learning English as a second language most often experience more worksheets than real books, more rote practice than exploration of ideas, more memorization than thinking (Kohn 2011).

The class had briefly worked with toy cars earlier in the year, so they have lots of ideas and share them freely:

You push it and it will go.
Toy cars need batteries to move.
You wind up a rubber band and then let go, and the car moves.
Toy cars need energy to move!

Sharon usually doesn't require students to raise their hand to contribute ideas or ask questions. Discussions are free-flowing conversations, and the students have learned, with Sharon's help, to listen, give eye contact to the speaker, and take turns. These are behaviors that are practiced often during the first six weeks of school, and learning them is an important part of the social curriculum and crucial to managing a group of students with a wide range of skills, behaviors, and language abilities.

Sharon tells the class that they'll have a chance to explore the toy cars that have been placed on the tables. "I want you to try to make them work, and then I want you to tell us how you made them work," she directs. "Write down your notes in your science notebooks." She asks the students to think about and give suggestions for how to treat the materials, and then facilitates an orderly transition by sending them off to experiment with the cars by dismissing one student at a time.

Engaging and Exploring

Whenever the students are engaged in experimentation, the room is transformed. An inquiry approach allows students to explore and discover science concepts through hands-on, direct experience. Inquiry also provides an authentic purpose for using language to learn about science. Engagement and language use is evident as children hunch over the toy cars that are placed on the table, trying things out, chatting with partners, and making discoveries. Sharon roams around the room, observing and asking questions. She doesn't tell students how to test things out, because she knows that good science teaching involves a limited, judicious use of information giving. Sharon does, however, help students talk about their learning, especially if they are English learners.

At one table, Benito watches as Alberto winds up a rubber band tighter and tighter before letting it go (see Figure 6.1). The toy car shoots across the table. Sharon asks him what made the car go. Alberto doesn't know the

Figure 6.1
Experimenting
with toy cars

word for rubber band, so Sharon provides him with the term so he can talk more precisely about his learning. Precision is important in science because it can ensure the reproducibility of experiments.

At another table, Cesar and Dao are trying to connect the batteries to wires to make the toy car move (see Figure 6.2). Cesar, who is very articulate and an identified gifted student, explains what he's doing. "You put the orange wire in the left upper corner and the green wire in the right lower corner, and that's how to make it go forward. And to make it go backward, you just switch them." Dao, who is much less proficient in English, is Cesar's "language buddy" and listens to his explanation before switching the wires to make the car move backward. Both boys cheer.

The students struggle and struggle to make the cars move, and their perseverance is impressive. At the front rug area, Trisha, Jackie, and Alejandra shine a big lamp on a toy car connected to a small solar panel (see Figure 6.3). They speculate about how much light the car will need to move. Jackie and Alejandra are shy and tentative; both were behind in reading and mathematics when they came to Sharon's school. In a more traditional setting that stresses rote learning, these students might never have been given the chance to think like scientists. Here, in an environment that supports critical thinking and provides opportunities to explore and experiment in small groups, the girls open up and develop their inquisitiveness and independence.

Figure 6.2
Cesar and Dao
are "language
buddies."

Figure 6.3
Experimenting
with a solar
panel

Another group is using an air pump and blowing on a little blue toy car, making it glide across the table (see Figure 6.4). Everyone is engaged, motivated, and involved in the science processes of observing, experimenting, predicting, communicating, recording, and hypothesizing. They'll share their discoveries during a whole-group discussion tomorrow.

Figure 6.4
Making a toy
car move

DAY 2

Making the Investigations Public

According to the National Science Education Content Standards (National Committee on Science Education Standards and National Research Council 1996), scientists develop explanations using evidence from their investigations and what they already know about the world. They make the results of their investigations public and describe them in ways that enable others to repeat them.

To provide a context for making students' discoveries public, Sharon begins science class by having the students assemble on the rug. With their notebooks in hand, partners talk about what they learned the previous day. As they talk, Sharon circulates, listening in on their conversations. When they finish, she calls them back and charts their ideas.

"Me and Diana pulled the red car back and then it drove," Jenn shares. Sharon asks the girls what they mean and has them demonstrate. Showing, rather than telling, can help beginning-level English learners communicate their ideas. Diana gets the red car and shows the class.

"What makes it go by itself?" Sharon wonders aloud, modeling inquiry.

"I think the wheels," Felicia speculates.

"Something must be in there that makes it go," John says. "But the blue car is different. If you pull it back, it doesn't go."

Sharon asks the class to think about the blue car and what makes it go. She calls on Carlos, who is normally a "tell me what to do and I'll do it" kind of student and would easily succumb to a steady diet of worksheets. During inquiry science, however, he comes alive and explains, "When you shine a light on the wire and the card thing [solar panel], it makes electricity, and then it makes the car go." Sharon has Carlos show the class the solar panel, which prompts a flood of personal stories. Kay saw one on television; Cesar's dad put solar panels on the roof of their house; Alejandra thinks *solar* is the word for *sun* in Spanish. All of these "self-to-science" connections are key to meaning making and could not happen if Sharon did not value and give students time to share their wealth of personal experiences.

The conversation moves to the car with the propeller, which prompts more stories about submarines, airplanes, and boats. "What makes the propeller go?" Sharon asks.

The Science and Engineering Practices emphasize asking questions.

"Electricity makes it go," Trisha says, "but where does the electricity come from?" This prompts the students to ask more questions.

What is inside a wire?

What does it mean to waste energy?

Where does electricity come from?

How does electricity turn on?

How does wind create power?

What makes fans go?

Sharon writes the questions on the chart and sends the students back to their seats with their journals to work independently and to try to answer some of the queries. As they transition back to their seats, Sharon gives the class feedback on their behavior by making statements such as, "I notice that most everyone is busy working hard to answer the questions you posed at our meeting," and, "I notice that everyone got back to their seats quickly and quietly." Reinforcing what students are *supposed* to be doing during inquiry science often prevents Sharon from having to remind or redirect individuals, especially those who are rambunctious and have a hard time focusing and working cooperatively with others.

Although understanding the concept of energy takes time, students' ideas are evidence that they have a sense of energy being transferred from one object to another. A rubber band can give energy to a car by pushing on it; a student can give energy to the rubber band by stretching it. In this way, much of the student reasoning reflects some sense of it being conserved: it starts somewhere (light shining on the solar panel), and it ends somewhere (the car moving). The students also have a sense of energy existing in different amounts. For example, you can give the rubber band more energy by stretching it, or you can give the solar panel more energy by shining the light on it for a longer period of time (Hammer, Goldberg, and Fargason 2012).

DAY 3

Planning Science Lessons

While planning a lesson, Sharon thinks about what support students will need to help them learn about the content or big ideas in the unit. She also thinks about the language that students will use to show her, orally and/or in writing, that they have met the content objective. Thinking about a language objective for each lesson helps her plan the support she thinks the children will need in expressing themselves in English. For example, for the lesson on Day 3, students will discuss the different sources of energy and then write about what they think energy is. Because Sharon knows that her students will need to *describe* where energy comes from and what it is, she plans to provide a written prompt to help them talk and write about their learning.

What Is Energy? Where Does Energy Come From?

"I've read your journals, and a lot of you wrote that batteries have energy," Sharon says as she begins the day's lesson. "Do we accept that batteries have energy?" Sharon does not want her students to believe everything they read or what they hear. She wants them to think critically.

"If batteries don't have energy, then they won't work," Felicia says. Dao repeats what she says, benefiting from Felicia's correct use of grammar and syntax. Benito also agrees.

"Anyone disagree?" Sharon asks.

"Batteries say 'energizer' on them, so they must have energy," John muses.

"You can recharge them," Cesar says. This opens up a flurry of chatter about how batteries work, different things that use batteries, and so on.

"So what is energy?" Sharon asks the class. "And where does energy come from?"

Sharon asks these "big questions" because she firmly believes that *all* children have the capacity to bring to the classroom a wealth of knowledge and experience. This contrasts with a deficit view, in which some educators have doubts about and low expectations for some communities of learners.

After a brief partner talk, the students brainstorm ideas about energy.

Water gives you energy.
I have a lot of energy when I ride my bike.
Things that have energy are hot, like a plug for a computer.
I use energy when I run laps.
I save my energy for when I get home.
I get energy from sugar and coffee.
You can save energy.
Kids have a lot of energy.
Drinks have a lot of energy.
Energy bars have energy.
Batteries have energy.

Power plants!
Energy comes from the sun.
The lights use energy.
Energy comes from a power company.

Some of the students' ideas show that they have a sense that energy comes in different forms (heat, light), comes from sources and can be stored (power plants, food, batteries, the sun, bodies), and can be used (for running laps, riding bikes). However, some of their ideas aren't technically correct in scientific terms. For example, the idea that "coffee gives you energy" isn't quite right: there are few calories in coffee (calories being units of energy). But to tell the class that the energy is really coming from the cream and sugar in the coffee, and that the energy from the cream and sugar really comes from molecules reacting with oxygen (Hammer, Goldberg, and Fargason 2012), would be inappropriate.

Energy, like "the whole of science . . . is nothing more than a refinement of everyday thinking" (Einstein 1936). Children's ideas about energy, like most science concepts, are refined over time by talking about and reflecting on their experiences in the world. Furthermore, it is not critical that every idea a child has starts out as scientifically sound. In fact, in some everyday contexts, an "unscientific" notion (coffee gives you energy) makes sense, whereas the "scientific" explanation seems absurd. "Imagine sitting in the café, hearing someone say, 'Coffee can't give you energy. It doesn't have any calories'" (Hammer, Goldberg, and Fargason 2012). What is more important is that students formulate ideas, support them, and refine them over time. This process of refinement is what leads to scientifically sound discoveries.

Sharon tries to help students organize their current thinking and experiences by creating a chart of energy uses and the sources of energy. She fills in the chart with students' ideas:

Uses Energy	Source (where it comes from)
TV	Wall/wires
Lights	From electricity/lightbulbs
Refrigerator	A plug in an outlet
Laptop	The charger/plug in the wall
DVD	Plug in the wall
Curling iron	Plug in the wall
Heater	?

Sharon brings an end to the discussion by posing a question for students to write about in their journals: What is energy? She sends the students back to their tables with the writing prompt "Energy is . . .," and they write with the enthusiasm of scientists who are trying to find out how the world works. Figures 6.5 and 6.6 provide a couple of examples of what they write.

Figure 6.5 "Energy is something that helps you get untired. Energy helps you get exercise."

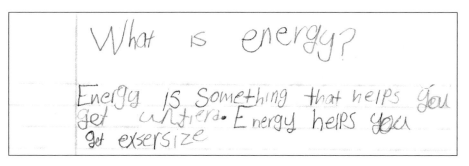

Figure 6.6 "Energy is some source of power that sometimes makes people active or for things that are not people. Energy just makes machines work."

DAY 4

Taking Stock of Student Learning

Each day after science, Sharon reflects on the lesson. She thinks about what went well, what changes she would make, the progress that students are making, and the next steps she will take. Her reflections are guided by her overall goals for instruction, which for this unit are primarily for students to think like scientists and use the scientific thinking processes to learn about energy. She also wants them to learn about energy forms and how energy is stored and transferred.

How does Sharon know what students know? By listening intently to their responses in whole-class discussions and partner talks, by reading their science journals, by observing them at work, and by hearing their responses to her questions and the questions posed by peers. She also asks herself questions about individual students. Are the lessons engaging enough for Cesar, Kay, Felicia, and John? Are these students getting the challenges they need? Are Jackie, Dao, and Diana getting enough language support so that they can understand the language of instruction and talk about their learning? Are the lessons differentiated enough to accommodate Mohammed and Brenda and their individualized education plan goals?

Evidence from their journals and class discussions informs Sharon that most of her students have beginning ideas about what energy gives us and where it comes from. Some, like John, Cesar, and Felicia, seem to have some sophisticated notions and quite a bit of prior experience and knowledge. Others, like Diana, are harder to figure out.

In her journal, Diana writes, "The energy is the plug." Sharon wonders whether her writing is a signal of a naïve conception about energy or a lack of proficiency in English makes it difficult for her to express what she knows. Or, perhaps Diana has limited experience with the concept because she's lived most of her life in Burma, where three out of four people do not have access to electricity. Sharon has learned not to make assumptions about the children in her diverse classroom. One thing that she does know is that all of her students need more experiences with energy, and that is exactly what she has planned for today.

Taking Apart Flashlights

It's cold outside, and the students file into the classroom, shivering. They gather on the rug, and Sharon starts rubbing her hands together. The students follow suit. Soon, everyone starts noticing that their hands are getting warm, and comments fly. Sharon models inquiry by asking why their hands are getting hot. "It has to do with science!" someone says. "It's energy!"

"Heat is energy!" someone else exclaims. Sharon tries to use real-life situations to contextualize learning.

"Today we're going to try to figure out how energy travels," Sharon begins. "You're going to take apart flashlights and try to figure out how the energy makes the lightbulb work." The students squirm with excitement as Sharon continues. "If I put a battery in the flashlight, how will the energy get to the bulb to make it work? Is there a little mouse that runs up and makes a fire so that the lightbulb works?" The students laugh. "It is an explanation, but not a good one," Sharon says. "I want you to try to come up with a good explanation of how the energy gets to the lightbulb, or how the energy gets to the toy cars to make them go."

The Science and Engineering Practices emphasize constructing explanations for science.

Sharon sends them off to work in groups of four and gives each group a poster on which to record and draw their ideas. Drawing makes communicating ideas easier, especially for beginning English learners.

As the children get to work taking apart the flashlights, they make a variety of observations. "I think metal has something to do with the energy getting to the battery," Alberto hypothesizes.

Figure 6.7
Taking apart
flashlights

Diana notices that the bottom of the flashlight is hot. "Ouch!" she says. "It's like when we rubbed our hands together." Sharon is pleased that Diana makes this connection. Benito explains to Trisha that the switch works by touching the lightbulb with metal.

A group of students is huddled around Sharon (see Figure 6.7). Kay notices that when she puts the batteries in and one touches the bottom part of the lightbulb, the flashlight works. Sharon asks, "Could you make the lightbulb work without the flashlight?" The children are skeptical. Mohammed is a student with autism who rarely says anything in class discussions. During exploration time, he opens up and comments, "If you put one battery in the flashlight, nothing happens; you need two."

Cesar is certain that the energy comes from the batteries, but he doesn't know how the energy gets into the battery. So many discoveries are happening! Benito observes that if you take the metal ring out of the flashlight, it doesn't work. Lots of students are noticing that things get hot when you use energy.

DAY 5

The Teacher's Role in Inquiry Science

Besides providing opportunities for students to interact with materials during experimentation, Sharon sees her primary role during science instruction as a facilitator. As children discuss, experiment, discover, and share their findings, Sharon listens and asks questions that help students deepen their understanding and think further about their learning. She summarizes students' ideas in order to highlight and make explicit important concepts that are being uncovered. And she provides language support to help children access the content and talk about their learning in English.

"Yesterday, many of you noticed that when you use energy, it gets hot," Sharon says, starting a whole-class discussion. "I went for a run this morning and it was cold outside. By the time I was finished, I was hot." This personal anecdote prompts a stream of comments and stories. Sharon just listens, asks questions, and summarizes as the children talk about their experiences with heat and how it relates to energy.

> **Student:** When you move, you get hot.
> **Student:** My computer and the iPod of my sister get hot.
> **Student:** My sister's curling iron gets hot.
> **Sharon:** Did you think about why it gets hot?
> **Student:** 'Cause you use them a lot, like the refrigerator.
> **Student:** My PlayStation 3 gets hot when we play with it for, like, three hours.
> **Sharon:** So things get hot when they use a lot of energy?
> **Student:** Because there's heat going through the wires.
> **Sharon:** Why is there heat going through the wires?
> **Student:** To make it work. Like cars don't start up if there's no heat.
> **Sharon:** So when things work for a long time, they get hot, like me when I was running.
> **Student:** 'Cause you're using your muscles. That's when you get hot.
> **Student:** I was watching a movie, and the DVD got hot after a while.

Figure 6.8
Experimenting
with toy cars

Sharon moves the conversation to the posters students worked on the day before and has different groups share. Cesar and Dao go first, demonstrating how their group got the toy car to move by connecting the wires to start the motor (see Figure 6.8). "You have to have the clip touching the metal part to make the motor go," Cesar says.

"Motors spin around and around and around," Sharon says, pointing to the revolving motor and contributing to the conversation just like one of the students. Felicia wonders why you have to put the clip to the wire to make the motor go. "'Cause it's metal," Benito replies. Joshua adds a story about jumper cables and how the energy moves from one motor to another. Students' knowing nods signal that they are making personal connections.

Another group shares their poster that has a statement and a question: "The energy comes from the batteries. How does the energy get into the battery?" Someone speculates that there may be liquid in the battery to give it energy, "'cause energy drinks give you energy." A third group finishes by describing how they got their toy car to move by connecting batteries.

DAY 6

Investigating What Makes a Flashlight Work and What Doesn't

Some of the "science" that students have been exploring has to do with electrical circuits. In an electrical circuit, electrons with a great deal of energy leave a source (in this case, a dry cell battery), move through a conductor (a wire), lose some energy in a load or resistance (a lightbulb), and return to the source. As long as the switch is closed (the wires are connected), energy is transmitted through the circuit. The lightbulb converts some of the electrical energy to light energy (Abruscato 2004). Rather than explain this process to her students, Sharon wants them to find out for themselves.

Sharon shows the students some flashlights that she cut open so that they can see inside them. She also shows the class several plastic zip-top bags that contain various materials she wants the students to use in today's experiments. Rather than telling the class how to treat the materials and the flashlights, she asks what they need to think about while using the science tools. When the ideas come from the children, Sharon finds, they are more willing to abide by the rules they make.

Holding one of the plastic bags, Sharon takes the materials out one at a time and asks the class if they know what each item is. She says its name, has the students echo it, and then writes the word on a class chart. In the bag are items like metal rings, metal screens, small plastic bags, wooden sticks, Styrofoam, wax paper, brass brads, rubber bands, paper, aluminum foil, and string (see Figure 6.9). Sharon explicitly teaches these words because she wants students to be familiar with them and be able to use them while experimenting. Later, when students have more experiences, she will introduce important science concept words such as *conductor* and *insulator*.

"Yesterday I heard a lot of you say that something has to be connected in order for the flashlight to work," Sharon reminds the class. "I want you to experiment with these materials, put them inside the flashlight, and connect them in different ways. Which ones make the flashlight work and which ones don't? Remember to make a prediction, or a guess, before you try something out."

The children disperse from the rug in pairs, excited to begin this new exploration.

Diana hovers over a battery she's wrapped in foil and then placed inside her flashlight. She's an independent thinker who thrives on the

The Science and Engineering Practices emphasize planning and carrying out investigations.

Figure 6.9
Test-objects
inventory and
materials

freedom that inquiry science allows. On her own, she gets out her science notebook and writes down what she's doing and what she's discovering. Diana sees an authentic need to keep track of her experimenting, and Sharon takes note of this as part of her ongoing assessment of her students' developing roles as young scientists.

There's a lot of chatter about which materials block the electricity and which ones allow the electricity to go to the lightbulb. Metal works, plastic doesn't work; try this—no, try that. The classroom has turned into a bustling science lab, and it seems that the children could go on all morning trying out their wonderful ideas.

What is powerful about inquiry science is that it gives all children, but especially English language learners, an authentic need and purpose for communicating their ideas. To provide support, Sharon will sometimes strategically pair up students with their language needs in mind. For example, she might place a beginning-level language learner with a more proficient student so that translation and linguistic modeling can happen. At other times, she'll place two students together who are at a similar language level so that both get more opportunities to talk. At other times, she'll let students pick their own partners.

After about twenty minutes of work, Sharon calls the students back to the rug to elicit their ideas and write them on the class chart:

Works	Doesn't Work
-Cover with metal stick	-Cover metal stick with wax paper
-Cover with foil	-Batteries the wrong way
-Cover with metal stick with wooden stick	-Silver between batteries
-Put gold ring between and on top of batteries	-Rubber band around the battery
-2 pieces of foam + metal ring + spring + batteries	
-Spring + bronze + battery + gold ring + battery	

DAY 7

What Will Make the Flashlight Work? Retesting Students' Ideas

Sharon displays the "Works/Doesn't Work" chart and asks the students to think about why some things made the flashlight work and other things didn't. She then has them turn and talk to a partner. When they are finished, Sharon asks for comments and questions.

Felicia says it's obvious that if the batteries are upside down, the flashlight won't work. Cesar objects to one of the statements on the chart and says that if you cover the metal stick inside the flashlight with a wooden stick, the bulb won't work. Alberto clarifies, adding, "He's saying you need metal or it won't work."

Figure 6.10
Visuals make learning accessible.

To illustrate, Sharon makes a quick sketch of a flashlight on the whiteboard (see Figure 6.10). "Inside, there is a metal spring, and from here up there's a metal stick," she says, pointing.

"Then we put the batteries inside here. The metal stick goes all the way down to the metal spring." Sharon asks Diana to get one of the broken flashlights so that she can show the class. Visuals and realia are helpful for English language learners, because they make concepts and explanations visible.

"When you move the switch, the little metal stick moves," Benito observes.

Sharon shows on her drawing what Benito is referring to, and the students' knowing nods serve as an informal assessment.

The Science and Engineering Practices emphasize asking questions.

Someone asks, "What would happen if you put one battery going up and one going down? Can the flashlight work with only one battery?" The students are beginning to ask more questions; it seems that their curiosity is boundless.

Carlos's Hypothesis

Recognizing that some students have new questions and that there is some disagreement about the statements on the chart, Sharon sends the class back to experiment further. She distributes the bags of materials from yesterday, and directs everyone to either double-check the ideas on the chart or pursue their new hunches. The students partner up and throw themselves into their experiments with enthusiasm. After about twenty minutes, Sharon calls them back to the rug to share a hypothesis that Carlos has formulated. As the students gather on the rug, Sharon writes Carlos's idea on a class chart:

If you put something metal between the batteries, then it will always work.

To finish the lesson for the day, Sharon introduces the word *hypothesis* as an "uncertain explanation until it is tested further," and has the students repeat the word to her. Pairing synonyms with academic terms helps make the content accessible for all students, but particularly for English learners. Sharon has the students think about whether they agree or disagree with Carlos, and tells the class they'll be exploring his hypothesis tomorrow.

DAY 8

How Should Scientists Behave?

Before school, several children from Sharon's class exaggerate when reporting how many laps they ran during runners' club. Recognizing this, Sharon begins morning meeting with a discussion about the cheating incident. She asks the class, "What does *integrity* mean? Talk with a partner about what you remember. You can use this sentence starter to help you." On the board, Sharon writes, *Integrity means* . . . She has the class echo the words before sending them off to chat.

Integrity is one of the weekly vocabulary words students studied several weeks ago. Sharon wants to use a real-life scenario and make a connection to science and ethics, illustrating that scientists, just like children, must be truthful in their reporting.

She calls the students back and elicits a few ideas.

> **Cesar:** John found a video game and turned it in to lost and found. He could have kept it.
>
> **Sharon:** So by turning it in, John was showing that he had integrity? [Cesar nods.] So by turning it in, John was being honest. *Honesty* could be a synonym for *integrity*.
>
> **Maria:** Like yesterday when we had a guest teacher. Kids could have gotten a drink after recess, but they didn't.
>
> **Sharon:** They were acting with integrity. They could have gotten a drink 'cause the guest teacher doesn't know the rules. But they did the right thing. Someone once told me that *integrity* means that you do the right thing even when someone isn't looking.
>
> **Benito:** Like sitting where you shouldn't be sitting when the guest teacher is here. You should sit where you should even when Ms. Fargason isn't here.
>
> **Cesar:** How does it compare to runners' club? [Sharon notices the connection Cesar makes.]
>
> **Sharon:** What do you think?
>
> **Cesar:** It's like some kids were cheating and they weren't being honest about their laps.
>
> **Sharon:** I have a question. Is it important for scientists to have integrity?

This question allows the children to reflect on the work scientists do. What if they say a pill will help my mom get rid of her headaches and it doesn't? What if they say a rocket ship is safe and it crashes? The students come up with their own real-life stories and questions. Sharon finishes the discussion by reminding the class that it's okay to make mistakes, or not do well, like when running laps. She asks, "What do scientists do when they make a mistake or when something doesn't work? Do they lie?"

"No!" the students respond. "They try something new!"

Weaving in discussions about honesty, integrity, treating one another with kindness, working cooperatively, disagreeing respectfully, and listening to one another is part of developing a community of learners, of scientists. It is part of the social curriculum that Sharon deems as important as learning academic content.

Exploring Carlos's Hypothesis

Sharon segues from the discussion about integrity to exploring Carlos's hypothesis. "When we were testing what worked and didn't work with the flashlights, we reported what happened and we told the truth. We had integrity." The students nod in agreement.

With the "Works/Doesn't Work" chart clearly in view, Sharon reminds the class about Carlos's hypothesis that as long as you put metal between the batteries, the flashlight will work. She then has the students pair up and talk to a partner about whether they agree or disagree with Carlos. To provide support for English learners, she writes a sentence stem on the board: *I agree/disagree with Carlos because* . . .

As partners chat and use their science notebooks as a reference, Sharon sits down with Diana and Brenda. Unlike John, Cesar, and Felicia, who are talkative and participate often in science discussions, these girls are quiet and hesitant. They are English language learners, and partner talks provide a safe environment for them to have a conversation. Brenda is at a first-grade level in reading and math, and because of this, she has an IEP. She needs a lot of exposure to a subject, and firsthand experiences help her make sense of what she's learning. Inquiry science has been good for Brenda because she has learned how to think for herself.

Sharon keeps a close eye on these girls, because sometimes they need structured support from her to say something about their learning. Sharon notices that the girls aren't saying anything, so she prompts them with questions pitched to beginning-level language learners, ones that can be answered with a yes or a no, with one or two words, or by pointing to a picture.

Sharon: Brenda, do you agree with Carlos?
Brenda: Yes.
Sharon: Why?
Brenda: I tried it.
Sharon: Point to the picture you drew in your science notebook.
   What did you put between the batteries, Brenda?
Brenda: The round metal thing.
Sharon: Say that in a complete sentence. I agree with Carlos because

   . . .

Brenda: I agree with Carlos because I put the round metal thing . . .
Sharon: Between . . .
Brenda: Between the two batteries.

After chatting with the girls, Sharon calls the class back together and elicits a nonverbal response. "Thumbs-up if you agree with Carlos's hypothesis and thumbs-down if you disagree." Nonverbal responses give language learners a chance to participate without having to produce language.

Next, Sharon asks for their thoughts and gets a flood of ideas. The students discover that pennies, dimes, brass brads, and aluminum foil all conduct electricity. This is a big idea that Sharon expects students will construct as they continue experimenting and reflecting. John jumps in with a generalization: "I guess brass, silver, and copper are all metal!"

"So do we all agree with Carlos's hypothesis?"

"No!" several students chorus.

"I object!" John exclaims. He explains that he put a red piece of yarn between the batteries and the flashlight worked. This prompts other students to chime in with their ideas. Raul says he put a piece of white paper between the batteries and the bulb lighted up. Joshua claims that when he placed a metal ring between the batteries, nothing happened. Some students have new questions. Kay, who often mulls over her ideas before she shares them, wonders aloud if the energy will get through if you put something thick between the batteries.

> The Science and Engineering Practices emphasize engaging in argument from evidence.

The Importance of Multiple Trials

There is a lot of confusion in the class and much disagreement. Sharon welcomes this kind of disequilibrium, knowing that it can motivate a scientist to explore further and think critically. Our brains want to attain equilibrium and make sense of what we are confused about. As usual, Sharon doesn't tell students what to do next, but asks them for their advice. "What should we do now?" she asks. "Some people tried something and it worked. Other people tried the same thing and it didn't work."

Several students suggest that they should try all the experiments again tomorrow, but all together this time, to make sure everyone agrees. As the lesson winds down, Sharon takes this opportunity to point out that when doing experiments, scientists try things over and over to make sure their conclusions are correct.

"We have to stop now," Sharon tells the class.

Benito moans, "Already!" In Sharon's class, this is a typical response when science time comes to an end. It's a response that she relishes.

DAY 9

Testing Carlos's Hypothesis Together

Sharon places the Works/Doesn't Work chart so everyone can see, and then holds up a flashlight. She always begins science class with a question. "Why do I want to check to see if the flashlight works the regular way before we test your ideas?"

Trisha, who has been participating in class discussions more and more each day, explains that if it doesn't work the regular way, something must be wrong with the batteries. Someone else chimes in that the bulb has to work so they'll know if their ideas are right or not. Sharon positions the batteries the "right way" and the flashlight works.

Sharon then prepares to test Brenda's idea that if you put one metal ring between the batteries, the flashlight will work. First she asks the students to put their thumb up if they predict it will work and their thumb down if they don't think it will. Nearly everyone thinks the flashlight will light, and sure enough, it does.

Sharon is constantly asking students what they think will happen, because she knows that children who are asked to predict the results of their experiments are more willing to change their thinking than children who function as passive observers.

Next, Sharon prepares to try out Raul's idea. He had disagreed with Carlos because he had put a piece of paper between the batteries and the flashlight worked. When Sharon asks Raul for the paper to try out his idea, she realizes that by "paper," he meant a thin piece of metal that looks like a piece of paper. Vocabulary is important in conveying your thinking, and although Sharon taught the students about the items in the plastic bags, Raul still needs more experience learning the words in English. Sharon asks for predictions from the students again and then tries Raul's idea, and the bulb lights.

"So far, Carlos's hypothesis is correct," Sharon says. She then proceeds to try a few more student ideas, and each time Carlos's idea holds.

Letting Student Thinking Guide the Lesson

Felicia suddenly asks a question that takes the lesson in a slightly different direction. Sharon keeps an open mind when teaching and often lets students' ideas and questions guide the lesson. These little "bird walks" often pay off and yield rich conversations that serve to deepen understanding and help students develop habits of mind or dispositions such as curiosity, healthy skepticism, and perseverance.

"What if you put the batteries in upside down?" Felicia asks. The other day she was convinced that the flashlight wouldn't work with the batteries upside down. Now she's not so sure. "Try it with the batteries upside down and with the metal ring in the middle of the batteries." Sharon is pleased with Felicia's willingness to take risks in front of the group. She is a very sensitive student who experienced many difficulties with her peers earlier in the year, crying easily when made fun of. Discussions during inquiry science have helped Felicia build her confidence and become a better listener. She now is able to evaluate, refine, and share her own ideas even when her classmates disagree with or challenge them.

Joshua follows Felicia's question with a prediction: "I bet the energy will go backward."

"Hmmm, I don't know," Sharon ponders, modeling inquiry. The students stare at her incredulously, not believing that she doesn't know the answer. Sharon notices this and responds, "Hey, when I say I don't know, I don't! We're all trying to figure this out together." When the bulb fails to light up, everyone is surprised.

Kay comes back to the question she had yesterday. "Put the batteries back the right way and put two metal rings between them. I wonder if the energy will go through if the metal is thick."

"I don't think so," John predicts. "The knobs on the batteries have to be touching, and if it's too thick, it won't work." About half the class agrees with John, others think the flashlight will work, and some are unsure. When Sharon tries it out and the bulb lights, there's excitement in the air, and everyone seems happy with the result except John. He remains skeptical, insisting that Sharon "must have done it wrong." Some children, like John, stick to their beliefs with a passion, even in the face of direct evidence.

"You saw it with your own eyes," Sharon says. "You try it!" She hands the flashlight and metal rings to John. He tries it and it works. "Now do you believe?" Sharon asks him. A grin grows on his face, and he seems convinced, finally.

Introducing Academic Vocabulary

Sharon sums up the experimenting, saying that "The only time the flashlight has worked is when the energy has gone through the metal." The children nod in agreement.

"While we were visiting the library this morning, Mrs. T., the librarian, said something about lightning and electricity." Sharon has the students turn and talk to a partner to help refresh their memories.

After a minute or so, she calls them back and asks for their ideas. Danny says, "If there's a lot of lightning, don't stand in your bathtub 'cause the lightning will come through the pipes and get you."

Alejandra adds, "And don't talk on the phone, 'cause the electricity will come through the wires and get you."

"You should stay away from metal," Maria chimes in.

"Yeah, the metal *lures* the lightning," Cesar says, showcasing his rich vocabulary.

"So it sounds like we have a pattern here," Sharon says, trying to sum up students' ideas. "When there's lightning, stay away from metal." She then writes two words on the board—*conductor* and *insulator*—and explains that a conductor is something that lets electricity go through it, like metal, and an insulator is something that keeps the energy inside. "A conductor is like the opposite of an insulator," Cesar muses.

"And stuff like rubber bands and paper are insulators, 'cause the electricity didn't go through them," Benito adds.

Sharon likes to introduce academic vocabulary in science at a point when she thinks students have had enough experiences to attach meaning to the words. She teaches some everyday words, such as *metal* or *paper*, ahead of time so that students can use them when describing their experiments as they learn. But Sharon worries that academic words, such as *conductor* and *insulator*, will have little meaning unless there is a network of ideas and experiences in which to embed the new terms.

DAY 10

Co-Creating Definitions for Big Ideas

After almost two weeks of instruction, Sharon thinks students have enough experience to attach meaning to key academic vocabulary. She builds on yesterday's discussion of the concept words *conductor* and *insulator*, introducing the following new words: *energy, source, stored energy*, and *energy action*. She writes them on the class chart, has the students say the words aloud together with her, and has them get into groups of four to discuss the first key word: *energy*. "What do we mean when we say *energy*?" she asks. "I'm not going to write down a definition until everyone has had a chance to think and talk with a small group. Then we'll come up with definitions together."

An inductive approach to teaching science is language intensive, and much of the talk comes from the students. They uncover big ideas, wrestle with concepts, and express the meaning of content in their own words as it unfolds over time. Sometimes, Sharon provides them with vocabulary to help them talk like scientists. At other times, Sharon and the students co-create definitions of these big ideas as a result of their experiences. As the students huddle in groups of four, they are intensely discussing what energy is; giving them the opportunity to think and express their ideas is very motivating.

After a few minutes, Sharon calls for the students' attention and begins a whole-class discussion. The students report that you can get energy from liquid, candy, juice, and batteries. Sharon responds, "You're telling me *where* you can get energy, but tell me *what* it is."

"Energy is power!" several students chorus.

"What is power?" Sharon asks, probing further.

"Something that gives you motion," someone responds.

"Is that always true?" Sharon asks. "What does the energy drink do for you?"

"It makes you do your job faster," Benito says.

"What other energy do we know?" Sharon probes. "You talked about batteries." The students chime in with all sorts of ideas. Batteries help you turn things on; they make things work; they turn lightbulbs on; you recharge a battery when it's dead to give it energy to work; you charge a cell phone from batteries to give it energy.

"How do we know if the toy car is using energy?" Sharon's questions nudge the students on, helping them tap their prior knowledge and experience during the unit.

"We know it works 'cause it moves!" someone exclaims.

"Raise your hand if you've ever run out of gas," Sharon says. "You get stuck on the side of the road and your family pushes your car and it moves, it works. Where is the energy coming from to move the car?"

"Your muscles!" the students answer in a chorus.

"So if it has energy, it works. If it doesn't have energy, it doesn't work," Sharon says, summarizing the students' ideas.

Just as she starts to write this definition on the class chart, John chimes in with an objection. "My dad gave me a robot and all the pieces were right, and I put energy in it and it didn't work."

The students all look at Sharon to see what her response will be. Although they are becoming more confident as scientists, they still think

Sharon has the last word. One of her goals is to get them to think of themselves as the keepers of the knowledge. "Can you put that one robot example out of your head for a minute?" she asks. John, the skeptic, nods. "Energy makes things work. Can you accept that?" Sharon asks him, genuinely interested in what he thinks. She's happy when students disagree and take a stand.

"Well, it makes things work *most* of the time," John grudgingly admits. Sharon smiles and writes this definition on the class chart: *Energy makes things work.*

Sharon proceeds with the next three terms in the same way. The students huddle in groups of four and talk about what they think the terms *source, stored energy,* and *energy action* mean. When they report on their discussions, they make all kinds of connections to the unit they've been engaged in and to their experiences in the world. When they are finished, the chart is filled with these definitions on the chart:

Energy makes things work.
Source is where you get energy.
Stored energy is when you save energy.
Energy action is when you use energy.

Finding the Big Ideas in the Materials

When they finish writing their definitions, Sharon directs the class to go work with the toy cars and flashlights. "Your main job is to think about the vocabulary words: Where is the *stored energy* and *energy action*? Where's the *energy source*? Think about these words, and think about where you see them in the cars and flashlights. And write down your thoughts in your science journals."

When the students get back to their tables, they dive into their experiments once again. This time, they document their observations in their notebooks (see examples in Figures 6.11 and 6.12).

DAY 11

Introducing More Formal Academic Language

Sharon begins science class by showing a videotape called *All About the Transfer of Energy* (Schlessinger Media 2000). The video highlights some of

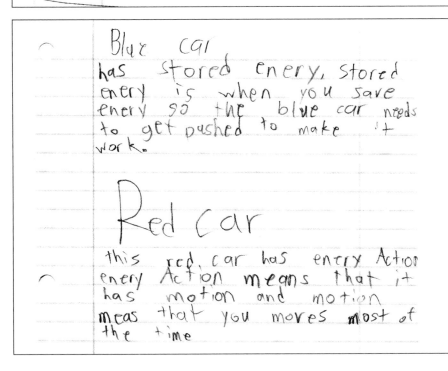

Red car
Energy action ← Red car
The wheels are moving they are ~~moving~~
energy action

Blue Race Car
The red Pump is the source because
the wind is how the car works.

Dump Truck
The Rubber band can be a source of
energy. Stored energy ⊂ ⊃

Metal car
The source is the motar and it's an
~~or~~ energy action.

Long Rubber Band Car
When you twist the black thing up it works it's a stored
energy

Figure 6.11
This student wrote about where the energy is stored and where the energy action is for each of the toy cars.

Blue car
has stored enery. Stored
enery is when you save
enery so the blue car needs
to get pushed to make it
work.

Red car

this red car has entry Action
enery Action means that it
has motion and motion
meas that you moves most of
the time

Figure 6.12
This student explains stored energy and energy action.

the big ideas that students have been learning about, such as *energy, source, stored energy*, and *energy action*. It also introduces more scientific terms for stored energy and energy action: *potential* and *kinetic* energy. When the video is over, Sharon has the class talk with partners about what they learned. She provides these sentence starters to help students who need a jump-start: *I learned . . . I wonder . . .*

When students are finished, Sharon pulls them back together and listens to their ideas. The discussion helps clarify and connect *potential energy* with *stored energy* and *energy action* with *kinetic energy*. Diana mentions that if you wind something up, like on one of the toy cars, it's potential energy.

Sharon uses the opportunity to get the wind-up car, and as she begins winding the propeller (see Figure 6.13), she says, "Diana's idea is that we're creating a lot of stored or potential energy here. We can see it . . . The rubber band is bunching up, twisting up. Can you see it?" She wants the students to "see" the concepts they have been learning about in the materials. Visual elements and demonstrations are especially important for English learners at beginning and early-intermediate levels of proficiency.

The class is riveted as Sharon winds up the propeller until it is so tight she can't wind it up anymore. Comments are flying about: It's getting bigger! It's bunching up! It's going to make the car move fast when she lets go! "What will happen when I let it go?" Sharon asks.

Figure 6.13 Demonstrations can help students "see" concepts in action.

"Kinetic energy!" students shout. "The car is going to move fast!" Sharon lets go of the car, and sure enough, the car zooms across the desk and onto the floor. The students cheer. Sharon then proceeds to demonstrate with the other cars, each time asking the students to identify where the *potential* and *kinetic energy* is coming from in the materials.

Identifying Testable Questions and Research Questions

Once she is finished with the demonstrations, Sharon asks for any further thoughts or questions. Dao, who was talking a mile a minute with Kay during their partner talk, shares a hypothesis with the class. This is surprising, because he rarely contributes to whole-class discussions. With his excitement spurring him on, he speculates that if you put a dead battery out in the sun, it will recharge. These aren't his exact words; Dao is an English learner who often rambles, repeats, and uses incorrect syntax. Sharon helps by rephrasing what he says, modeling correct usage.

"Could we test Dao's hypothesis?" Sharon asks. The students are excited and want to try it out. Cesar raises some doubt and doesn't think Dao's idea will work, but he has another idea. "I think I can *upgrade* Dao's idea," he says. "Attach a dead battery to our solar panel and then put it out in the sun. I think that will recharge the battery."

"I wonder what's inside a battery," Diana says.

"When you have a question or hypothesis, like Dao and Cesar, you can answer it by testing it or by talking about it," Sharon explains. "We'll try out their ideas tomorrow. But sometimes you might have a question like Diana's that's either too dangerous or not possible to try out, and then you have to ask a scientist. Those are called research questions."

Sharon tells the class that her science professor will know the answer to Diana's question. She gets out her computer, and the class helps her draft an e-mail to Professor Goldberg:

Dear Professor Goldberg,

We really want to know what's inside a battery. We are very curious, but we can't try it out because it's not safe. Since you're a smart scientist, we are asking you. Can you tell us what's inside a battery? Can you send us an explanation or can you help us find an article on the Internet?

Sincerely,

Room 13

As science class winds down, Sharon directs the children to get out their laptops and do a Google search to see what they can find out about batteries. As Sharon searches on her own computer, she finds out that in fact, scientists in Japan have recently invented a battery that can be recharged by the sun. The researchers are calling their concept the Light Catcher, which is basically a photoelectronic battery made up of tiny antireflective solar cells that soak up energy from the sun.

Cesar and Dao were on to something after all! Their wonderful idea was allowed to form and be shared because they are in a classroom where children's voices are nurtured and waiting to be heard.

DAY 12

Testing Cesar and Dao's Hypotheses

Sharon begins science class by reviewing Cesar and Dao's hypotheses about recharging dead batteries, and showing the class the four dead batteries she brought for the experiment. She asks Felicia to try out the batteries in a flashlight to make sure they are dead. Sharon then asks the class how they'll go about testing Cesar and Dao's hypotheses. "How will we conduct our experiments?" she asks. Rather than tell them, Sharon leaves it up to the children to decide. She turns the thinking and decision making over to them as much as possible.

Diana suggests that they leave one dead battery out in the sun for five minutes and then get it and see if it works. Sharon tries to elicit other ideas, but no one presents one. Cesar volunteers to hook up a dead battery to the little solar panel using wires and tape. Kay volunteers to make a "Do Not Disturb" sign to place next to the experiments. Sharon sits back and lets the students decide how to manage the science. All of a sudden, Cesar jokes, "Hey, if my idea works, I want the money!" Everyone laughs.

Providing Language Support

When everything is ready, Sharon leads the class outside to set up the experiment, and then brings them back in to wait. In the meantime, she elicits predictions from the students, offering two sentence frames:

> *I predict _____ hypothesis will work/won't work.*
> *I predict _____ hypothesis will work/won't work because _____.*

After briefly turning and talking to a partner, the students share their predictions. Some think both will work because "the sun will give energy to the batteries." Others disagree, challenging the notion that the sun can get its energy into the batteries. After about five minutes, Sharon has two student volunteers get the batteries. Once the batteries are back, someone suggests that Felicia put both of them together to see what happens. The excitement in the room is palpable: all eyes are fixed on Felicia. She tries it, and the bulb doesn't light.

"Now what should we do?" Sharon asks. Someone suggests that Felicia put one good battery and one dead battery in the flashlight. The result: a faint glow from the bulb. The class is stumped. Is the good battery doing all the work? Or did the dead battery get recharged a little and start doing some of the work also? Joshua thinks they should leave the battery outside until the end of the day, and everyone agrees.

Although Sharon knows quite a bit about different aspects of science, it's not necessary for her to know all of the answers. What's exciting for her is learning right along with the students, genuinely modeling inquiry. To finish up science class for the day, she asks the students to think about ways we can get energy other than from batteries. The students offer their ideas: the sun, wind, oil, and muscles. And with each idea, they share their lived experiences, contextualizing and bringing meaning to science.

DAY 13

What's Inside a Battery?

The students are excited because Sharon tells them that Dr. Goldberg has responded to their e-mail. In his note, he refers the class to a website that explains what is inside a battery, and then gives the students directions for making their own "lemon battery."

Sharon shares information from the website Explain That Stuff (www.explainthatstuff.com/batteries.html). As she shares, she paraphrases and uses illustrations (Figure 6.14) to make the explanation more accessible to her students. "All batteries contain one or more cells," she says. "But people often use *battery* and *cell* to mean the same thing. A battery has three main parts: a positive terminal, a negative terminal, and a liquid or solid in between called an electrolyte. When a battery is connected to an electric circuit, a chemical reaction takes place that creates an electric charge."

Figure 6.14
Parts of a
battery

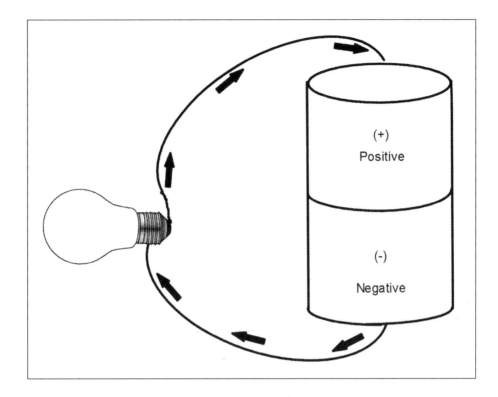

Sharon knows that explanations, especially ones about concepts that involve things the children cannot see (the chemicals inside the battery), can be difficult to understand. But the students are mesmerized, and impressed that a real scientist has answered their question. They nod with familiarity as Sharon refers to the battery's terminals, and a few are thrilled to find out that there really is liquid inside (sometimes), just as they thought.

The Science and
Engineering Practices
emphasize developing and
using models.

Next, Sharon shows the class the materials she's gathered for them to make their lemon batteries. Students wiggle with excitement as they read the directions.

To find directions for making a lemon battery, go to http://pbskids.org/zoom/activities/sci/lemonbattery.html.

Making Lemon Batteries

Following a set of procedures is an important part of doing science, and making a lemon battery is a perfect way to give the students this experience. The class divides into four groups, and Sharon distributes the lemons, copper wires, paper clips, pennies, scissors, and digital clocks. She moves from group to group, helping cut the slits in the lemons and making sure that the materials are being used safely. The students are excited and work hard to follow directions, and after about a half hour, two groups actually make the digital clocks work! (See Figures 6.15–6.17.)

Figure 6.15 • Making lemon batteries

Figure 6.16 • Making a timer work using a lemon battery

Figure 6.17
Working
together to test
the lemon
batteries

DAY 14

Summative Assessment of Student Learning

Over the course of three weeks, Sharon has formatively assessed her students' learning by listening to their ideas during partner talks, and small-group and whole-class discussions. She's read their science journals, and she's observed them at work as they experimented with toy cars, flashlights, and lemon batteries. Formative assessment has allowed Sharon to gauge the effectiveness of her instruction along the way, and to get a pretty good idea of how students are progressing toward the goals of the energy unit: for students to learn how to act and think like scientists, and to learn about different forms of energy and how it is stored and transferred.

Despite the confidence she has in her ongoing, informal assessments, Sharon still feels nervous when she gives the Energy Unit Assessment and the District Science Benchmark Test. Will the students rise to the occasion? Have they really learned the content? The stakes are high, and Sharon knows that if her students don't do well, criticism will surely follow from important stakeholders such as parents, administrators, school board members, and other teachers. More important, it is her students that she's concerned about. Sharon knows that they need to learn how to demonstrate their knowledge in informal *and* formal ways, and be prepared to break through the barriers that have kept underserved students from excelling in math, science, and technology, which are the gatekeepers to higher education.

But every year her fears turn to relief and then to joy as she pores over the results, which show that her students have indeed learned the content. On the Energy Unit Assessment, most of her students are able to name three energy sources and three examples of stored energy, and respond well to several open-ended questions about energy transfer (see examples in Figures 6.18 and 6.19).

On the District Science Benchmark, nearly 75 percent of Sharon's students score as either "advanced" or "proficient," with only three students scoring below "basic." And although these are scores to be proud of, Sharon does not allow the assessments to be the sole driving force that guides her instruction. High-stakes, standardized tests narrow the scope of what's considered worthwhile learning. Rather than developing long-term, high-level thinking skills, students and teachers are increasingly focused on doing whatever it takes to pass the test (Ohanian 1999). For poor and minority students, this emphasis on testing rather than good teaching

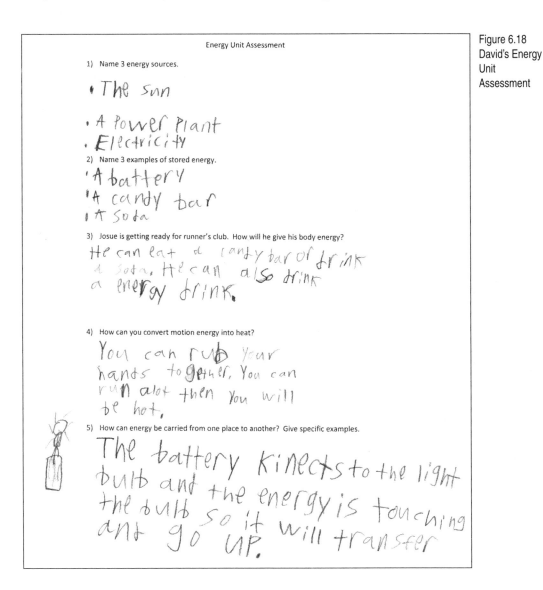

Energy Unit Assessment

1) Name 3 energy sources.

• The sun

• A Power Plant

• Electricity

2) Name 3 examples of stored energy.

• A battery

• A candy bar

• A soda

3) Josue is getting ready for runner's club. How will he give his body energy?

He can eat a candy bar or drink a soda. He can also drink a energy drink.

4) How can you convert motion energy into heat?

You can rub your hands together. You can run alot then you will be hot.

5) How can energy be carried from one place to another? Give specific examples.

The battery kinects to the light bulb and the energy is touching the bulb so it will transfer ant go up.

Figure 6.18
David's Energy Unit Assessment

means an erosion of the very practices that are most effective (Houk 2005). Instead of sacrificing good teaching in order to produce better test scores, Sharon lets good teaching lead the way.

Figure 6.19
Juan's Energy
Unit
Assessment

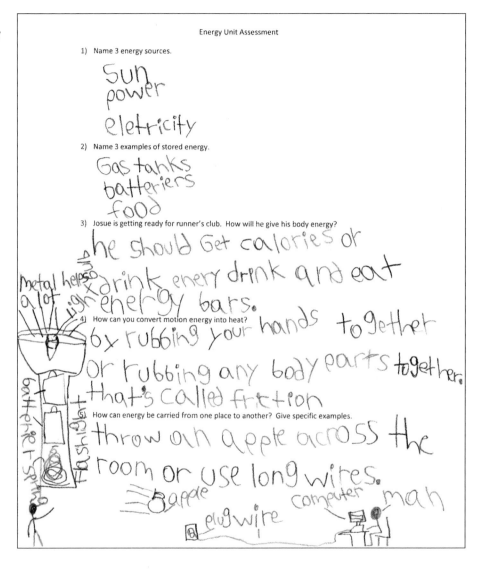

Energy Unit Assessment

1) Name 3 energy sources.

Sun
power
eletricity

2) Name 3 examples of stored energy.

Gas tanks
batteriers
food

3) Josue is getting ready for runner's club. How will he give his body energy?

he should Get calories or
drink enery drink and eat
energy bars.

4) How can you convert motion energy into heat?

by rubbing your hands together
or rubbing any body parts together.
that's called friction

5) How can energy be carried from one place to another? Give specific examples.

throw an apple across the
room or use long wires.

CHAPTER 7

NAVIGATING THE CHALLENGES OF INQUIRY SCIENCE: RESPONDING TO TEACHERS' QUESTIONS

When teachers engage their students in inquiry science, they actively involve them in questioning, discovering, and investigating. They help develop their students' critical-thinking skills as well as their attitudes toward science so that they will be curious, skeptical, and open to modifying their explanations. Teachers focus on essential concepts in science rather than on having students memorize bits of information. And they bite their tongues when they have the urge to explain and lecture, thereby allowing their students to do the thinking and the talking.

These best practices are important for all children, but essential for underrepresented minority students, who are often denied a thinking curriculum. Yet even for students from upper-income schools, the focus of science education is often reduced to memorizing facts rather than understanding and applying big ideas. A teacher friend of mine who works at an affluent school bemoans the fact that when her students enter her fourth-grade class, they are great at digesting and regurgitating science information, and they do really well on standardized tests. But when it comes to designing experiments, explaining reasoning, or asking their own questions, they are miserably unprepared.

In his book *The Global Achievement Gap*, Tony Wagner talks about the gap in education that goes beyond the disparity between the quality of schooling most middle-class kids get in America and the schooling available for most poor and minority students. Wagner asserts that a global achievement gap exists between the schooling our children receive now and what they'll need to succeed in today's (and tomorrow's) global knowledge economy (2008). Today's employers are looking for people who can engage in discussion and ask good questions, and these are the skills inquiry science helps students develop.

When school districts commit to using an inquiry approach to teaching and learning science, the results can be rewarding. For example, the Science Advisory Blue Ribbon Task Force for the San Diego Unified School District, one of the largest and most diverse urban districts in California, recommended that the district "continue with efforts that have proved effective and successful over the past 5 years, including the use of inquiry-based education and hands-on programs" (Science Advisory Blue Ribbon Panel 2009, 3).

Inquiry science can be an effective way to teach children how to behave like scientists. It can even yield higher test scores, as evidenced by large urban districts such as San Diego, Los Angeles (Lawrence Hall of Science 2012), and Detroit (Geier et al. 2008) that have embraced such an approach. But is teaching inquiry science easy? Teachers face many challenges when they move away from their science textbooks and move toward an open inquiry approach. How do teachers facilitate discussions, and how do they learn to ask good questions? What do they do when children take little "bird walks" or change their minds in the middle of a thought? How do they respond when their students want to "Google it!" to find the answer, rather than explore and think on their own? Do they accept any answers from students, even the ones that are scientifically incorrect? How do they get their students to support their claims with evidence and explanations, like adult scientists do? How do they incorporate engineering practices into inquiry science? And how do they meet the needs of a diverse group of learners, especially when individual students have special learning needs and goals?

In this chapter, Sharon answers questions that teachers ask about inquiry science by drawing on her experiences while coaching Becky McRae and Melanie Speros, two third-grade teachers at Sharon's school who have chosen to take the leap into inquiry. To show teachers how to meet the challenges that inquiry science poses, Sharon uses examples from Becky and Melanie's diverse classrooms as they navigate through a unit on the sun, moon, and stars. Using examples from classrooms with nearly 100 percent underrepresented minorities is particularly important because they show that inquiry not only can thrive in such environments, but is essential for students who have been traditionally left out of the pipeline that leads to opportunities in the fields of science, technology, engineering, and mathematics (STEM).

QUESTIONS & ANSWERS

Q: I have heard the term inquiry used quite a bit lately. It seems that many publishers and programs say that they are inquiry based. I don't want to reinvent the wheel if something great is already out there. How can I tell if the program I am already using is inquiry based?

A: As we mentioned in the introduction, there are several different kinds of inquiry, some more open than others. The type of inquiry or the science program you are using is less important than the scientific practices the students are using. The framework for the Next Generation Science Standards says that focus should be put "on important practices, such as modeling, developing explanations, and engaging in critique and evaluation (argumentation), that have too often been underemphasized in the context of science education" (National Research Council 2012, 59). When using any curriculum material, it is important to ask what the students will be doing and be responsible for and what the teacher will be doing. Are the students responsible for the explaining, or is that left to the teacher or the textbook? If you notice that many of the important practices are left to the teacher, think about how you can rework the explorations to place the responsibility on the students. For instance, an experiment that is included in a science textbook to explain a scientific phenomenon can instead be used as a common experience that the students use to make their own hypotheses, or to explain the cause of what they have observed.

From the Classroom

The district-adopted science materials that Melanie and Becky were using in their classrooms asked that students go outside and observe the movement of the sun across the sky. The students were to go outside at different times of the day, point to the location of the sun in the sky, and record the data on a worksheet provided by the textbook. At the end of the day, the students were to notice that the position of the sun changes throughout the day, and the teacher and the textbook were responsible for explaining why this happens.

Both Melanie and Becky incorporated this activity into their teaching, but they altered it so that the students, rather than the teacher, did the scientific practices. They took their classes outside at different times of the day and noticed that the sun was in different places. Melanie and Becky told stories of their eyes hurting and having to squint as they drove east to school in the morning and again as they drove west in the afternoon. And then they asked the students to think about why those things happened. "Why do you see the sun in different positions in the sky?" they asked. The students worked on explaining this and made arguments and critiqued the reasoning of others. They used models to explain and test their ideas. Becky and Melanie had transformed the textbook lesson into an inquiry-based activity to help their students engage in important scientific practices.

Q: When my students are involved in a debate about a scientific idea, they frequently ask if we can look up the answer in a book. When is it appropriate to do some reading? Adult scientists have to do a lot of reading!

A: In school, science education often depends upon reading, and many students are used to depending on sources such as textbooks or Internet sites to provide them with information. Although reading is an excellent way to gain knowledge, it must be done in the right way so that the information is meaningful to the student.

Most adult scientists spend a portion of each day reading scientific papers and research about the topic they are studying, and they are very purposeful about what they read. They don't look at any book that seems to be lying around their office. They read to answer questions. Has this research already been done? Has someone else made a discovery that might help me think about my research more clearly? Is there more I need to know about my topic before I start testing something? These questions in scientists' minds help guide their reading and tell them when they have read enough or need to look more closely. They also help the reader decide when to employ questions to assist with comprehension. Since scientists are reading for a clear purpose, they can easily decide when they should go back and read something again, look up unknown vocabulary, or talk with someone about sections that are still unclear. Since they have specific questions that need to be answered, they know they should read carefully until everything makes sense to them.

This is how students need to read also. They need to open their textbooks with curiosity and have specific questions they want to answer. Unfortunately, students are often told what they are about to study and then told to turn to the portion of the textbook that discusses that topic. Sometimes the students have a "hands-on" experience and then turn to the textbook. The problem is that many times, the students are doing the reading because the teacher told them to. And since many teachers are much more knowledgeable about literacy than science, they skillfully guide the students through comprehension of the piece. However, the students often don't know what they are reading for. They are missing the purpose.

The goal of inquiry science is to make students think and behave like scientists. It is to build curiosity so that when they read, they are reading for a purpose and want to comprehend the material to satisfy their curiosity (see Figure 7.1). Inquiry science seeks to build learners who are always asking themselves, "Does this make sense to me?" And when it doesn't make sense, we want learners who say, "Wait a second. I still don't get it." This is what is going to drive them to truly understand the science they are reading about.

The problem with much of the scientific reading students do in school is that it is helping them prepare for a test rather than to become thoughtful, curious scientists or human beings. These skills are critical in the twenty-first-century workforce. Additionally, students need to be able to analyze and evaluate the information they are reading, instead of only absorbing it. When students engage in inquiry before reading, they are learning to be curious and to ask questions, and when they enter into a text with their own questions, they will begin to analyze their reading for what is valuable to their understanding and what leaves them with more questions. As Christy Pedra, the president and CEO of Siemens Hearing Instruments, says, "If you want to encourage young people to be scientists, it's not how much they can retain, but how much they can explore. It's how you ask the next question. I can look up anything, but I can't take it to the next level without pushing and exploring" (Wagner 2008, 6).

Figure 7.1
Reading for a
purpose

From the Classroom

When Becky McRae opened up her science unit with the question "Where does the sun go when it sets?" many students were excited to share their initial ideas. "It goes into the ocean." Or, "It switches places with the moon!" The students were excited to tell the rest of the class what they thought and eager to draw diagrams that put their thoughts on paper. However, once there was some debate among the students, many of them asked if they could look up the answer in a book. While two students were engaged in a lively debate about whether the earth spins or the sun and the moon switch, one student exclaimed, "Can't we just Google it?" Becky validated his question by telling the students that reading is a great way to get information but that she wanted him and the rest of the class to think about what made sense to them before they read about what made sense to others.

The students spent two more weeks proposing ideas, making models to test them, collecting data, and listening earnestly to each other as they shared. They became interested in much more than the sun. They talked about shadows and how they are created. They wondered about the moon and why the pattern it follows is different from that of the sun. And they were extremely curious about why the moon has different shapes and why you can often see the moon during the day.

At this point Becky chose to present some other sources to her students. She first carefully selected one clip from a video about the moon and introduced it to the students.

"I am going to show you a video that shows what scientists have discovered about the moon. They have been collecting data about the moon just like you have, but they have been working for hundreds of years. It's really important that we keep our brains on when we watch this. No one should watch this like you watch cartoons on Saturday morning. We can't just stare at the screen. We have to think and wonder and try to get our questions answered. We have to ask ourselves, 'Does that make sense?' and stop and think when it doesn't."

Becky then asked the students to tell a partner about a question they had that they were going to watch for in the video. Some students wondered where the moon gets its light, and others were curious about what causes the different shapes that they see. After a couple of students shared their questions, she played the clip and the classroom came alive. There was an excited buzz as the students watched. They quietly exclaimed to their partners as their questions were answered, and they participated in a lively conversation when it was over.

The class talked about this clip for two days, and when they all decided they understood it, Becky introduced some nonfiction reading to the class. The students noticed a diagram they didn't understand, and Becky allowed them to spend some time trying to figure it out (see Figure 7.2). She didn't explain it to them. She asked them to talk it out and guided them through it with questions.

The students wondered why there were two sets of moons and why the inner circle looked the same at every phase. One student said, "Well, I know there aren't two moons. But I don't know why the picture shows two sets." Then another noticed that half of each moon on the inner circle was lit up and that this matched the side of the earth that was lit.

"Why do you think that is?" Becky asked. The students talked together and decided that this was because the sun was shining on one half of the earth and the moon. They looked and talked more and decided together that the inner moon is what you see from space: the sun is always lighting one half. The outer circle is what you see from earth: the moon's orbit allows our eyes to see only part of the side of the moon that is lit, and this causes the different shapes that we see each day.

The students in Becky's class were ready to engage in scientific reading. They had questions that they desperately wanted answers to and were willing to put in the work to understand what they were reading or watching.

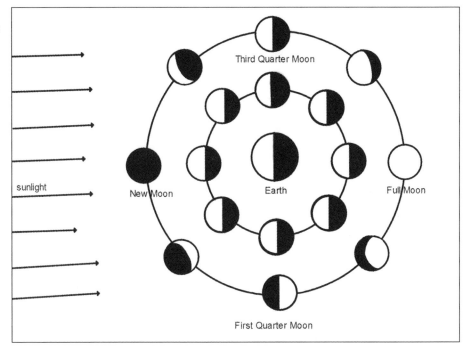

Figure 7.2
It's important to
let students
make sense of
diagrams.

sunlight

Third Quarter Moon

New Moon

Earth

Full Moon

First Quarter Moon

Becky knew she had introduced reading at the right time, and she was delighted with her students' engagement and excitement. Several read more books on their own time and had conversations with their families about what they read. They came back to school eager to share about these things with the class.

Q: My students often change their minds when they are sharing their ideas. I sometimes call on individual students to explain their thinking and they talk about an idea that is different from what they said previously. It makes it really difficult to get anywhere in a conversation. What should I do?

A: It is common for students to change their minds frequently during inquiry science. Much of this has to do with the fact that they are adjusting to an inquiry approach to teaching. Students are usually not asked to answer a difficult question until they have been given the answer in some format. In fact, much of the time when teachers ask questions to tap students' knowledge and experience, they are often really asking, "Do you know what I know?" or "Do you know what *scientists* already know?" This question makes invisible the culture, the home, and the knowledge of our students, especially those who are marginalized and who traditionally have not had their voices heard (Delpit 2012). These students are not used to formulating their own viable scientific ideas.

In inquiry science, students are learning to create their own answers based on their thoughts and observations. This is not easy, and it may cause them to be uncomfortable for quite some time as they adjust to the different ways their ideas are being evaluated. No longer is the teacher confirming or denying their responses; instead they are being asked to justify and make sense of the things they are saying. Children often feel nervous when other students share different ideas or disagree with what they have shared. This leads many of them to change their minds.

Teachers must take a large role in solving this problem by choosing their words, actions, and tone of voice carefully. Once the students learn that you value their ideas even when they are wrong or others disagree, they become more confident and stick with their thoughts until they have a good reason to change their minds. Teachers can also solve this problem by asking students to write or draw their ideas in a notebook or on a poster to share with the class. This helps them commit to one idea, and helps the teacher keep track of who is saying what. When writing or drawing, students should be encouraged to back up their ideas with evidence so that they see that when the reasoning behind their thoughts is sound, they should not change their minds until they hear something that convinces them otherwise.

Students can help each other construct viable arguments and stick to them, and teachers can facilitate that by putting them in small groups to talk or asking them to share in pairs (see Figure 7.3). A child is much less likely to feel intimidated while sharing ideas with a small group than when sharing with the entire class. However, it is imperative to teach these groups how to work together and to make the expectation for talking and listening clear. (For classroom management suggestions, see Chapter 3.)

From the Classroom

As Becky started teaching the earth, moon, and stars unit, she noticed that although students were excited to share, their answers were often incomplete, consisting of just fleeting thoughts. One person would share an idea and then change his or her mind to agree with another idea shared right afterward. Becky noticed that students were having trouble making sense of anything because no one would stick to one topic. She asked the students to work in groups and create a poster that answered her initial ques-

Figure 7.3
Students can
help each other
construct viable
arguments.

tion: where does the sun go when it sets? She told them they could either write or draw and asked that each member of the group play a part in deciding what went on the poster. As the students were working, she moved among the groups and talked with them. Here, she asked the students to stick with their ideas and work together to justify them and explain to other group members how they made sense. She validated reasoning that made sense instead of answers that were correct. One student shared that the sun sank into the ocean when it set because she had seen it happen while visiting the beach at night. "I've seen that too!" Becky exclaimed. "Put that on your poster."

As the student wrote, another thought out loud. "Well, I'm not quite so sure about that."

"Why not?" Becky asked.

"I'm not sure. It just doesn't make sense to me that the sun sinks into the ocean."

Becky asked the group to think more about the question as they continued to work on their poster. They put a question mark next to their idea so that they would remember to ask the rest of the class about it when they shared with the whole group. Later, when the class worked through this question together, the students shared their ideas confidently and didn't change their minds so frequently. They were starting to trust their own ideas.

Q: *What do I do when I am in the middle of a science lesson, get stuck, and don't know what to do next?*

A: Teaching inquiry science can be difficult, because teachers might not follow their lesson plans step-by-step. And each class session cannot always be planned out minute by minute, because it is impossible to know exactly what questions students will have or what they will become interested in. But it *is* helpful to plan each day's lesson by thinking about where the students are. What productive steps are they taking toward understanding a bigger concept, and what can you do, as their teacher, to help them take more steps in the right direction?

Even with the best-laid plans, there may be times when you just feel stuck in the middle of a lesson. If that happens, it is okay to take a minute to think and regroup. Thinking about your next moves while managing the class can be very difficult. Asking the students to talk with a partner can give you a quick moment to think, and if you need more than a moment, you can ask them to take out their science notebooks and write down their thoughts about a certain scientific question they have been pondering. This will give you a chance to collect your thoughts and will allow the students to process their ideas at the same time. Ideally, you will all come back with clear minds and be ready to tackle the important issues at hand.

Oftentimes, it is helpful to meet regularly with other teachers who are doing inquiry science. Even if these teachers are not working on the same topic you are, they can listen and offer perspectives and advice about your next steps in the short term and the long term. Talking with other teachers about where you have been and where you're going can give you new ideas that will help guide your daily planning.

From the Classroom

Melanie Speros's class had spent several days trying to understand why the moon appeared during the day and in different shapes. They had collected observations, proposed ideas, and created models to test their hypotheses. However, they weren't able to come to a consensus about anything. During one class period, the students seemed to be spinning their wheels. They had several ideas on the table but couldn't find a way to prove any of them. Melanie knew what they needed to know but didn't want to give them the information. She was afraid that as soon as she started handing out facts, the students would stop being the curious and thoughtful scientists they had learned how to be. But she didn't know what to do with the fifteen minutes of class time that was left either. She asked the students to choose a question they had been exploring (Why does the moon appear in different shapes? Why does the moon appear during the day but the sun never appears at night? Where does the moon's light come from?) and then write or draw about it in their science notebook. She instructed them to write a paragraph that would help prove the accuracy of their idea to a neighbor. While they were writing, Melanie used the time to talk with some of the quieter students so that she could find out what they were thinking as well.

After school, Melanie and Becky met to talk about the struggles they were having. Although their students were in different places, they both thought they had gotten to a point where the students were going in circles. Both of them felt frustrated and confused with what was happening in their classes. It eased Melanie's mind to know that she wasn't the only one with this problem, and she and Becky worked together to carefully plan a sequence of readings that would give the students new information to use when problem solving.

Q: *What do I do when the students seem to get the correct answer right away?*

A: It is not uncommon for students to appear as though they know the right answer in the beginning of a science unit. They often see information in a book or watch informational videos that give them facts they often bring up in class. It can be discouraging when you have planned a compelling question to ask to launch an investigation, only to have students answer the question correctly on the first try. However, it is important to ask students to give you more than their initial correct answer. Asking them to justify their thinking or prove to you that what they know makes sense can reveal holes in their understanding. Additionally, there are probably many students in the classroom who are interested in thinking about the question but are intimidated because those who just gave an answer seemed very confident.

In *Classroom Discussions: Seeing Math Discourse in Action*, Suzanne Chapin, Catherine O'Connor, and Nancy Anderson describe several teaching strategies that can help students move beyond their initial responses, deepen their reasoning, and engage with their classmates' ideas (2011). (For descriptions of these strategies, see Chapter 2.) Having students (or the teacher) rephrase or revoice what others have said, encouraging them to add to what their peers have shared, or asking them to agree or disagree and explain why pushes students to examine and explore science concepts. And providing sufficient wait time after asking a question can help students expand on their ideas before sharing them.

From the Classroom

When Melanie asked the class her opening question, several students in her class responded very quickly. "The sun doesn't go anywhere! It stays in one place and the earth spins."

After several students had agreed, Melanie asked if there were any other ideas they would like to share. No one responded, but instead of confirming that the earth spins, she asked the students for justification.

"Can you tell me why that makes sense?" she asked. The students' reasoning soon illustrated that they had some factual knowledge but lacked the conceptual understanding that Melanie desired.

"My second-grade teacher told me," one student shared.

"I saw a video on the Discovery Channel," another added.

"Okay," said Melanie. "Let's make sure that we can prove it. Scientists always make sure they understand why something happens." One student shyly raised her hand and quietly added that she always thought the sun and the moon switched places.

"I agree!" shouted several others.

"Can you say more about that?" Melanie asked. The student shook her head anxiously, but Melanie assured her that it was okay to take her time. "I really want to hear what you have to say," she said in a patient voice. "We can wait."

Melanie's class had been working on wait time in other subjects, so her class waited patiently for almost a minute as the student put together her explanation. Finally, the student answered. "I know when it is daytime here, it is nighttime in China. So I think that we are seeing the sun and they are seeing the moon. When we're ready to have nighttime, the moon comes over to us and the sun goes over to them."

Melanie drew a picture of what the student said on the whiteboard in front of the classroom (see Figure 7.4). As she drew, she rephrased what the student had said. "So, you mean that the sun travels from here to here [as she showed the sun traveling around the earth from North America to China], and the moon comes around the other way when they switch? Is that correct?"

Figure 7.4 Illustrations can make students' thinking visible.

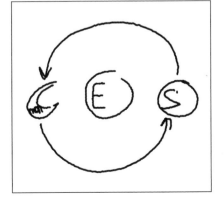

After the student confirmed, Melanie asked for more clarification. "Do they switch really fast, like one-two-three switch, or are they moving slowly and gradually?" Melanie's interest in the student's idea gave the girl increased confidence, and she gladly stood up and modeled with her hands how she imagined the sun and moon moving. Melanie wanted to involve the rest of the class in this idea, but instead of asking whether they agreed or disagreed, she asked them if this new idea made sense to them. Now, even the students who had originally shared the "correct" answer were thinking about this idea, and several of the classmates debated about which idea made more sense and why. Later in the unit, the class came to an agreement that the sun, in fact, did not move and that day and night happen because the earth rotates. However, the work that they did helped the students form and communicate sound reasoning to back up this claim. They no longer said that they knew because their second-grade teacher told them. They were able to give empirical and logical evidence.

Q: Do I accept any answer that a student gives during inquiry science?

A: A scientist wouldn't provide an answer to a question without an explanation or justification, and neither should our students. So when we are given an answer during inquiry science, it's important that we ask for evidence or an explanation, whether the answer is scientifically correct or not. For example, a child who is trying to explain where all his Christmas presents came from, and who shares the belief that Santa and his elves brought them in the middle of the night, may have evidence to back up his beliefs. Perhaps the cookies that he left out were nibbled away, or a piece of red felt from Santa's pants was left in the fireplace. He may even have seen "from Santa" written on the gift tags under the tree. In this case, the child's argument is a good one, because he has evidence to back it up. Of course there are several counterarguments to the child's explanation. For example, how could Santa make that many toys and deliver them to that many kids all in one night? But because the child's idea is backed up by evidence, it merits further investigation—investigation that could lead the child to discard his naïve conception or belief.

Sometimes students (and adults) give answers that seem wonderful but are lacking any explanation or evidence. For instance, if a teacher asks where water goes after it has been left out for days, many students would say that it evaporated. Although this answer is correct, it does nothing to explain what really happened to the water. Similarly, students may repeat things that they have heard or read without really understanding the concept. For example, when asked why one ball rolls down a ramp faster than another, students often say that it is because it has more energy despite the fact that they don't really know what energy is.

Although we know observation can be a fallible teacher, it is important to encourage students to use their experiences and observations as evidence when providing answers. That way, their ideas can be held up to examination and experimentation.

From the Classroom

Becky asked her students why we have different seasons on our planet. One student exclaimed, "It's because of the solar system!" This was not an adequate answer, because it did not provide an explanation for the seasons. However, instead of ignoring the student, Becky asked him to clarify his answer and share about how the solar system caused seasons. The student paused for quite some time and then shared that he had seen a book in which all the planets were pictured circling around the sun. The picture made him think that a planet's orbit had something to do with the seasons. This was a good answer, because it gave an explanation to Becky's question, and it was backed up with evidence, which led the students to talk more about the earth's orbit and to think about why the orbit might create the seasons.

In Melanie's class, a student shared that the sun would always shine on you more if you wore black or were holding a sandwich made with American cheese. Melanie grinned and then asked the student to explain his answer. He said that when he was wearing black T-shirts, he was always hot and could feel the sun beating down on him. Then he said that one time the cheese in his sandwich melted when he was outside in the sun. "Do you think the black shirt and the cheese made the sun shine on you more?" Melanie asked. The student thought, and then decided that black definitely made the sun stronger. Black always made him feel hot, and when he touched the dark seats in his car after it had been sitting in the sun, he always got burned. Although the idea that black makes the sun stronger is incorrect (black actually absorbs the majority of light energy wavelengths), accuracy is not necessarily what gives merit to a scientific idea. What's important here is that the student was providing evidence. And by examining the evidence, the student eventually recanted his statement about cheese. Grinning, he shared that the sun had made his sandwich melt, but he didn't think the cheese was at fault. By asking her student to provide evidence and an explanation for an answer, Melanie was able to help him think like a scientist and recognize one of his naïve conceptions.

Q: I'm worried about my students who have special learning needs. Can you give some examples of how teachers have addressed individual student needs during inquiry science?

A: Inquiry science provides many opportunities to differentiate instruction and address students' diverse learning needs. These opportunities extend to those students with learning disabilities who continue to experience a science achievement gap when compared with students with no disabilities (Next Generation Science Standards Writing Team 2012).

The idea of "inclusion," however, goes beyond meeting the needs of students with learning disabilities. Inclusive educators are responsive to all learners, and as they plan a science lesson, they prepare from the outset for a wide variety of aptitudes, needs, and interests. In their article, "Differentiating Instruction for Disabled Students in Inclusive Classrooms," Alicia Broderick, Heeral Hehta-Parekh, and D. Kim Reid propose that inclusive education "seeks to resist the many ways students experience marginalization and exclusion in schools." The authors posit that "inclusive education is fundamentally about *all* students, and the full spectrum of challenges of public schooling—around issues of poverty, second language acquisition, racial and ethnic discrimination, disability, etc.—must be attended to for education to be inclusive" (2005, 195).

Many students with special learning needs have individualized education plan (IEP) goals that are directly related to conversational or communication skills. One of my students, for instance, was struggling with his ability to relate and empathize with other students; his IEP goal read, "The student will take speaker and listener roles in conversation by talking about a partner's interests." I often worked with this student on his ability to have friendly conversations with others, helping him ask appropriate questions. He learned how to ask someone how his or her weekend was, and to give a reply that was appropriate to the answer. I found that this student could also work on his goal during science time. Because he had difficulty attending to what others were saying during science discussions, I worked with him to develop a signal (touching his back) that encouraged him to actively listen to the speaker and respond to what he or she was saying during our class discussions.

Many other students have IEP goals that are related to behavior. One of my students with autism was having trouble spending time on task. His

IEP goal was to increase his time on task to 70 percent by the end of the year. After getting to know the student, I learned that he loved reading nonfiction books and was able to obtain an impressive amount of knowledge from them. In fact, once he noticed the condensation that had formed outside my water bottle and pointed it out to me. "Wow!" I said. "I wonder where that came from." His eyes lighted up as he told me that he knew exactly what it was. It was water from the air in the classroom that had collected on my bottle. Then he ran to the nonfiction section of our classroom library, found a book, and in no more than ten seconds, turned to the page that described condensation. It was amazing. I decided to use his love of books to encourage him to spend time on task listening to others and completing the work he was supposed to do. I gave the student a timer and taught him how to use it. We agreed that he would keep it and set it at five-minute intervals. For five minutes, he would be expected to do whatever the rest of the class was doing. If he touched another student or picked up anything off the floor, he would have to set his timer back. When he completed the five minutes, he spent another five minutes reading a box of nonfiction books he had selected. I gradually increased his time on task as he got more comfortable with the expectations. During inquiry science, he sat still during class conversations and often shared the information he had learned from his reading. His contributions gave the class new evidence to think about as they were trying to make sense of things, and they often looked forward to the profound tidbits he would share.

Inquiry science offers several formats for students to work on IEP goals. For those who have speech-related goals, the oral, conversational parts are ideal times to do this work. Students who have content-specific goals can work on them during independent or group exploration or work time. For example, one student from a special day class was mainstreamed into my classroom during science instruction. The student was working on a physical science–related goal to meet an alternative performance assessment standard, specifically designed by the state for students with moderate to severe disabilities. Her IEP goal was to "sort magnetic from nonmagnetic objects." While the other students in my class were working on experiments with their magnets, I quickly set up a sorting task for this particular student that allowed for a modification in instruction. After observing her work for a few minutes and documenting her progress, I sent her off to work with the other students so that she would have the same opportunities for learning as her nondisabled peers. It is important that during inquiry science (and for all subject areas), teachers presume that *all* students are competent and capable of benefiting from academic content (Broderick et al. 2005).

Although some students will need instructional modifications to meet alternative performance goals, inquiry science can also accommodate students with less severe disabilities because it offers multiple modes of representing content such as graphic organizers, hands-on experiences, discussion, journaling, reading, and models. These instructional features can provide the support these students need to work around their disabilities and reach the same performance expectations as their nondisabled peers.

From the Classroom

Melanie has several students in her class with speech IEPs. More specifically, several of her students are working on specific articulations they have trouble with. Although these students see a speech teacher twice a week to help them with their articulation, Melanie also helps them during her science time. She will preview academic vocabulary before a lesson and look for words that might be challenging for them and for which they might need support. Melanie also uses students' mistakes as opportunities for the class to practice talking about vocabulary or important ideas. For example, one student with a lisp shared that the sun looks like it is moving because the earth spins. Because of her lisp, she mispronounced the word *spin*. Without embarrassing the student, Melanie highlighted this word as an important vocabulary term and told the students to talk with a partner about what *spinning* means and why it is important. While the students talked to each other, she met with the student to model the way the word should sound and showed her where to put her tongue when she said it. Afterward, Melanie asked the class to share their ideas and then taught them the academic term and synonym *rotate*.

Becky has a student with a language-processing disorder in her class. The student has an IEP goal that calls for her to respond appropriately to open-ended questions, given repetition and proper wait time. When her students share important ideas, Becky makes sure to ask several kids to repeat what was said. She often says, "Wait—I don't quite understand what you are saying yet. Can someone else say it in a different way?" For the student with the IEP, it is extremely beneficial to hear important ideas over and over, as it enables her to join in and restate what other students have said. However, the rest of the class benefits from this as well. They learn that it is okay to be confused and that when they are, they should speak up. The students learn to be comfortable asking each other to clarify their words or add to what has been said in order to make these ideas more comprehensible.

Q: *The Next Generation Science Standards place a big emphasis on engineering. Will I be able to incorporate engineering practices if I am teaching inquiry science?*

A: The framework for the Next Generation Science Standards lists eight practices that are essential for science and engineering:

> *Asking questions and defining problems*
> *Developing and using models*
> *Planning and carrying out investigations*
> *Analyzing and interpreting data*
> *Using mathematics and computational thinking*
> *Constructing explanations and designing solutions*
> *Engaging in argument from evidence*
> *Obtaining, evaluating, and communicating information*
> (National Research Council 2012)

These practices are essential to the spirit of inquiry science. It will be easy to incorporate engineering into your inquiry-based classroom since the same practices are required there, although the students perform them for a slightly different purpose. In science, scientists seek to learn about a phenomenon. (For example, what causes cancer? What is creating the hole in the ozone?) In engineering, engineers use the same eight practices to create a product that will solve a problem, meet a need, or fulfill a desire. (How can I cure cancer, or how can we repair some of the damage already done to the environment?) For elementary students, engaging in the science and engineering practices prepares them for the important work they will do as future scientists.

Although engineering tasks are built into the Next Generation Science Standards, it is easy to incorporate the engineering design process into your classroom in other ways. For example, my students used engineering and the design process to solve a real problem in our classroom. I would not allow them to use pencils in the classroom because I detested the horribly loud noise created by the pencil sharpener. After defining this as a problem, the students used the eight practices to brainstorm and create prototypes for a quiet pencil sharpener (see Figure 7.5). During the process, they used mathematics and computational thinking as they measured the decibels of each design (using an application on my cell phone) and found the differences from the original pencil sharpener. Additionally, they researched the science behind how machines work.

Figure 7.5
Designing a
quiet pencil
sharpener

Other types of engineering tasks are easy to incorporate into the class-room. Structural engineering tasks, such as designing a bridge to hold a certain amount of weight, are common activities for elementary school children. However, the framework for the NGSS says that it is also impor-tant for students to have the opportunity to do "projects that reflect other areas of engineering, such as the need to design a traffic pattern for the school parking lot or a layout for planting a school garden box" (National Research Council 2012, 70). These kinds of projects can be implemented in the classroom by having students design, and then improve upon, class-room rules and procedures. For example, my students designed a way to decrease pushing and shoving as they all crowded around a computer cart at the end of the day to plug in and store their netbooks. Although I prob-ably could have designed a system for them to use, I helped the students use the engineering practices to design, test, and redesign a model that solved our problem in an efficient way. These projects are challenging, engaging, and fun for students, and they provide them with opportunities to apply the engineering practices.

From the Classroom

Melanie and Becky wanted to create a way for their science classes to build a sense of community since their group comprised students from three dif-ferent homeroom classes. They knew that building a sense of community would help the students feel safe about taking risks later when studying the earth, moon, and stars. So they implemented a ball-and-ramp challenge for everyone to participate in. Each group of students had to create a ramp from materials they found in the classroom (whiteboards, books, rulers, and so on) that would make a ball of their choosing travel the farthest. As groups created their ramps, they considered many variables: the size of the ball, the effect of the friction created by the ramp's material, the steepness of the ramp's angle, and so on. The students completed the design process together and in doing so, learned to listen to and support one another. During the final competition, the students cheered for their own design but also commented on other ramps, noticing things their peers did that may have helped the ball go farther. This engineering activity was a successful way to help students begin using the eight important science practices while also helping to create a safe environment for student learning during inquiry science.

Q. Is there ever room for teaching students scientific facts or information during inquiry, or is inquiry science only about asking questions?

A: Effective science teaching involves a balanced focus of instruction between science information, concepts, and investigations (California Commission on Teacher Credentialing 2008). Even during inquiry science, students sometimes need to build background knowledge, especially if they have limited experience with a concept, and providing students with information and facts can help with this. At other times, students need to go to an outside resource for information, such as books, the Internet, or a scientist. For example, during a unit on energy (see Chapter 6), my students were curious about what is inside of a battery. Because opening up a battery isn't safe, the class wrote an e-mail to Dr. Goldberg, a physicist friend of mine, and asked him to help out. In a return e-mail, Dr. Goldberg told the class about an Internet site that provided the students with lots of information and facts about batteries. The students were thrilled about what they learned, mainly because they had been experimenting with batteries for several weeks, and had many questions that they were curious about. They already had a network of ideas in which to embed this new information.

During inquiry science, providing information and facts still has its place, but it happens in a different way. For example, when Melanie or Becky find themselves needing to teach by telling, they are more strategic and judicious about their information giving, especially if what they are telling short-circuits students' own initiative and investigation process (Zemelman et al. 2005).

From the Classroom

Melanie knew her students would be taking the upcoming district science test, so she wanted to provide them with practice thinking through test-type questions in the same way they had been making sense of each other's questions throughout the unit. On the interactive whiteboard at the front of the room, Melanie projected a *Jeopardy!*-style game board (see Figure 7.6).

Hidden beneath each dollar amount was a science question for the class to think about. A student would choose a category, then a dollar amount, and then the class would try to answer the question. The first question read, What are three facts about the sun? Before taking the leap into open inquiry, Melanie would have called on a student and elicited an answer without any discussion. Now, she elicits an answer and then has the students talk with a partner about whether they agree or disagree. This strategy challenges students to think more deeply about what they are learning and changes the activity from a simple recall of facts to an exploration of ideas. So when Melanie called on a student to give a fact about the sun, the student responded, "The sun is a medium-sized star. I read it in *The Magic School Bus*."

"Thumbs-up if you agree, thumbs-down if you disagree," Melanie said. "Now turn to a partner and talk about why you agree or disagree." The room erupted in conversation, and the discussion was fascinating. Some students agreed because they'd learned about the fact while watching television. Others disagreed because "The sun is humongous! How could it be

Figure 7.6
Melanie's
Jeopardy!
Game Board

Sun	Moon	Stars
$100	$100	$100
$300	$300	$300
$500	$500	$500

a medium-sized star?" Another student clarified that "It's medium *compared* to bigger and smaller stars, but it looks humongous to us because it is the closest star to earth." And so the conversation went on—students going back and forth, sharing their ideas, while Melanie listened and facilitated the discussion until there was a consensus.

A SHIFT IN THINKING

Melanie and Becky report that they've experienced a shift in their thinking about teaching science. They talk less and listen more. They encourage children to think, reason, argue, elaborate, ponder, and question. And they have noticed that their students' thinking has shifted as well. No longer are students giving one-word answers or sitting quietly and believing everything they hear or read. They are more actively engaged, more skeptical, more invested. Although Becky and Melanie know that presenting facts and information is sometimes important, and that explaining still has a place, they also realize that teaching by telling doesn't ensure that their students will understand. Inquiry science has reinforced for them that meaning making is the key to learning, whether the topic is reading, social studies, mathematics, art, or science. It is what Paolo Friere refers to in his book *Pedagogy of the Oppressed*, where he writes about the need for both the teacher *and* the student to engage in a dialogue where both learn, reflect, and participate in meaning making as they "read the world" (1970).

CHAPTER 8

DEEPENING TEACHERS' SCIENCE CONTENT KNOWLEDGE THROUGH INQUIRY

Educational researchers have proposed that teachers must have an understanding of subject matter content and employ effective teaching strategies to teach well and make ideas accessible to others (Shulman 1986). One is not sufficient without the other. Although we have stressed throughout this book that a teacher doesn't need to be an expert in science or know all the answers to students' questions to teach from an inquiry approach, knowing and understanding the concepts that one has to teach *is* important. In fact, studies have shown that teachers with stronger content knowledge pose more questions and are more likely to have students pose alternative explanations, propose more investigations,

153

and pursue unanticipated inquiries than teachers with weaker content knowledge. Furthermore, teachers with weaker content knowledge tend to engage in more direct instruction, telling students the content rather than having them explore and find out for themselves (Alonzo 2002).

If teachers possess an inaccurate understanding of the science content they are expected to teach, they are unlikely to make scientific ideas accessible to their students. For example, researchers studied a group of preservice teachers and their content knowledge of the phases of the moon (Trundle, Atwood, and Christopher 2006). They found that before engaging in professional development, most of the teachers, like the children they were preparing to teach, did not understand the cause of the moon's phases. Initially, when asked to recall what they knew, they remembered only fragments of knowledge, and some held naïve conceptions, thinking that the moon's phases are caused by the earth's shadow. But after engaging in inquiry during a course about physics for elementary teachers, the teachers' understanding of the phases of the moon improved dramatically, and it wasn't because they were told or had the phases explained to them. They collected data by systematically observing the moon each night, drawing what they saw, and then coming back to class to participate in "sense-making discussions" with their peers. They drew diagrams and used models to explain their ideas. In the process, they were able to disprove common misconceptions about the moon's phases based on their own discoveries. The instructor acted as a facilitator, asking questions and setting up opportunities for the teachers to move through the inquiry process. Inquiry helped these teachers construct scientifically sound explanations for the moon's phases, and by the end of the class, they were ready to teach their students from an inquiry approach.

Not everyone has the opportunity to participate in the kind of professional development experiences described above. So how do teachers deepen their science content knowledge so that they can become more effective while teaching science? Participating in professional development is definitely one way. But teachers can also learn about content by engaging in the inquiry process on their own, or with colleagues and friends. In this chapter, Sharon models a process she goes through to better understand what she's about to teach. This process is the same one she has her students experience as they seek to make sense of the world around them.

SEVEN STEPS TO DEEPEN SCIENCE CONTENT KNOWLEDGE

Below are seven steps I use for planning and deepening my own content knowledge. Although I usually follow these in order, the process is not always linear, and some of the steps (especially toward the end of the list) become somewhat circular as my understanding and insights produce more questions.

1. Start with a Content Standard

Content standards tell you where to start in your planning. They give you a good idea of what students should know and what they will be tested on later. Decide which standard or standards you are going to teach, and do your best to unpack them so that you truly understand what they are saying.

2. Define What Your Students Need to Know

I like to know exactly what my students are going to be responsible for at the end of the unit. I check out released questions from the state test and look at questions from previous district tests. I want to know what the questions will look like and what the students will need to know. I don't do this because I am going to "teach to the test" or deliver the answers to these questions. I make sure I define what students need to know so that I can effectively adjust my itinerary. If I know that students need to end up in certain places, my ears become attuned to their responses and questions that might help us go down that path. And if the students aren't going down the right path on their own, I know I need to bring something up or ask a good question to get them going in that direction.

3. Self-Investigate

Once you have an idea of what students need to understand, do your own investigation of the content you are going to teach. Think about what you already know and understand and how it makes sense to you. Then, make a list of the questions you have about the content area. This is sometimes difficult to do after reading the standards, which often tell us what information we need to know. However, do your best to go beyond the words. Do you actually understand the concepts behind what they are saying?

Where do you observe this content in your life? What is intriguing about it? What else do you want to know? What is still confusing to you? What could you do to figure out the answers to these questions? When thinking about what you already know about the content and brainstorming questions, a Know, Wonder, Learned (KWL) chart can be a useful tool (see Figure 8.1 later in this chapter).

Sometimes, when it is difficult to come up with your own questions, doing some reading can be a good place to start. This gets your brain thinking in different ways and reminds you of all the different parts there are to the topic you are teaching. However, when you read, don't accept all the information at face value. Be an active reader and make sure that what you're reading actually makes sense to you. Try to match the information to what you have observed in real life, and note questions when there are parts that still don't make sense.

Once you know what questions you have, start investigating. There are many things you can do to gain content knowledge. Books and Internet resources offer a wealth of information. Reading can help you get your questions answered in a timely fashion. Videos are also a great resource for quick information. My favorite investigation method is to set up a study group of people who will engage in the inquiry process with me. They can be other teachers, friends, or family members who are interested in the topic you are teaching. You can meet formally or bounce ideas off each other at the dinner table or during your recess duty.

4. Plan for Naïve Conceptions

Think ahead about what students might think and say about the topic you are teaching that, although not correct, might make sense to someone making observations in the real world. Make a list of the merits of these ideas. In what ways might they actually be valid? Then, think about why they are naïve conceptions. Why are they invalid? Is there something that can be observed to prove or disprove the idea?

5. Formulate a Compelling Question

Gather up all the questions and discoveries you have made, and put them together to come up with a question that will inspire your students to do the same amount of thinking you did. Think about this one question for a while, and run it by other people if you can. Your opening question can really make students curious, which will get your unit going in the right direction.

6. Anticipate Student Responses

What do you think students will say after you ask the opening question? Try to anticipate their answers. Make a list of what students might say and what evidence they might have for their ideas.

7. Think Through Responses

Once you have anticipated student responses and naïve conceptions, you can begin to plan how to respond to these ideas. What will you say to students to inspire critical thinking and keep communication going? It is impossible to plan for every scenario, but thinking ahead helps you expect the unexpected and tunes your ears in to what is important.

Each day, you will need to repeat Steps 5 through 7 to plan what to do for the day. Think about what you will say to open up the lesson. Maybe there is a question left unanswered from the day before, or maybe you have a question based on something you were exploring. Before you begin the day, take a minute to predict what the kids might say and plan for how you will respond. This planning will help you be successful with each lesson, and even though you don't know exactly what will happen, it will help you feel confident.

WORKING THROUGH THE PROCESS WITH OTHER TEACHERS

Recently, I sat down with a group of student teachers to help them plan a unit they would be teaching on stars. They started by looking at the standards. Since the Next Generation Content Standards were not yet adopted, they decided on one of the California Earth Science Standards: "Students know the patterns of stars stay the same, although they appear to move across the sky nightly, and different stars can be seen in different seasons." We looked at the end-of-the-unit test from the district-adopted curriculum materials and found several multiple-choice questions that were directly related to this standard. The unit test posed the following questions: What is a constellation? Why do stars appear to move across the night sky? Why do you see different constellations in the winter and in the summer? After looking at the standards and reading the unit test questions, it was clear to all what the students needed to know about stars.

I asked the student teachers to close their notebooks and think about stars themselves. I asked what they were curious about and what they thought was intriguing about the stars. This seemed to be much more difficult than looking at what students needed to know. The student teachers repeatedly went back to the standards, saying things like, "Well, they need to know what a constellation is" or, "They need to know that the constellations aren't moving, but the earth is spinning, which makes them look like they are."

"These standards are important," I said. "But let's put them aside for now. When you think about stars, what do you think is important and what do you wonder?" I waited through several seconds of silence and then someone offered a tentative question.

"What are stars made of?" she quietly asked.

"Good question," I said. "What else?"

"How many stars are there?" someone added.

Another offered, "Why do you see different constellations in different seasons? I know that's what the standard says, but I'm not quite sure why."

"Wonderful!" I said. "Let's think about that one together. What do you think?"

We had a long conversation about the night sky and why we observe certain things, and the student teachers shared their questions about what the standards really meant.

This conversation helped us think about things the students might also wonder. Where do the stars go during the day, and why can't you see them when the sun is out? If the sun is a star, how come it looks so much bigger than the rest of them? We were also able to predict where the students might have naïve conceptions. We thought that many would think that stars traveled around the sky since you could see them at some times and not at others. One of the student teachers remembered that someone had shared the idea that all the stars come together and form the sun. Although we knew this wasn't true, we also knew that it made sense in a way. Early in the morning, you can see millions of stars, and they seem to gradually disappear as the sun comes out. We could understand why students might think that the stars become the sun.

We worked together to come up with an intriguing opening question that we hoped would get the kids talking and wondering. We settled on telling a true story: "Mrs. McRae and Ms. Fargason like to run together early in the morning before school. One morning, Mrs. McRae noticed the Big Dipper right over her house, and pointed it out. They ran for an hour, and when they got back, the Big Dipper wasn't there anymore! The stars were really hard to see, but it definitely wasn't over her house anymore. What do you think happened?"

We thought about what kids might say in response to this story. They might say that the stars traveled to a new location or that we just missed them because it was so hard to see. We thought that some would provide the correct answer: that the earth rotated, so the location of the stars in the sky changed.

We used these ideas to plan for some possible next moves in case any of them came up. We found a time-lapse video that showed stars moving across the night sky in case the students needed some visual evidence to back up the story they told, and we thought about appropriate responses to the answers we predicted the students would give. This lesson was ready to be taught, despite the fact that it was not a step-by-step plan, and the student teachers were successful because they had planned using the inquiry process.

PLANNING AND GAINING CONTENT KNOWLEDGE WITH THE NEXT GENERATION SCIENCE STANDARDS

The following example is provided to demonstrate how you can plan an inquiry unit using the Next Generation Science Standards (NGSS). Although this example is specific to the NGSS, it is important to note that you can use the seven steps with whichever set of standards you may be using.

1. Start with a Content Standard

For this example, I will discuss one of the third-grade life science standards: *3.IVT Inheritance and Variation of Traits: Life Cycles and Traits*. This standard has four disciplinary core ideas within it, which can cover the following topics: Growth and Development of Organisms, Inheritance of Traits, Variation of Traits, and Natural Selection. Specific information about the content of these topics can be read in the NGSS standards.

2. Define What Students Need to Know

The NGSS have performance standards built in, making it easy to see where the students need to be at the end of the unit. The performance expectations are color-coded and tell you what the students need to be able to do (Scientific Practices), know (Core Ideas), and generalize (Crosscutting Concepts). The performance expectations for the 3.IVT standard are as follows:

3-LS1-a.
Construct explanations from evidence that life cycles of plants and animals have similar features and predictable patterns.

What Does This Performance Standard Mean?

Although it is true that some animals such as the beetle and the butterfly have similar life cycles, things that do not appear similar follow similar patterns as well. For instance, humans experience the same process of birth, growth, reproduction, and death as plants do. However, plants have different names and definitions for their life cycle. In most living things, the next stage of life can be predicted by looking at the current stage. Tiny animals and plants will grow bigger, and when they have reached adulthood, they will likely reproduce. Vocabulary changes, but the life cycle is an umbrella that connects all living things.

What Experiences Might Help Children Understand These Ideas?

Growing plants and watching small animals grow are examples of projects that students can do to observe life cycles in action. Bean plants, when properly tended and given time, can go through the entire cycle. Additionally, moths and butterflies will complete the life cycle in time for a class to observe the entire process. Many students come to class with a wealth of knowledge about life cycles because they are highly observable in the real world. To encourage inquiry, have students construct explanations about the similarities between life cycles by using their observations as evidence, rather than merely naming each phase.

3-LS3-a.
Use evidence to support explanations that traits are inherited from parents, as well as influenced by the environment, and that organisms have variation in their inherited traits.

What Does This Performance Standard Mean?

We inherit some traits from our parents. For example, my parents gave me my hazel eyes, and a baby giraffe has his parents to thank for his long neck. However, even when we inherit traits from our ancestors, there is a great variation between them. I have hazel eyes, whereas my brother's eyes are blue. Cats from the same parents can have a wide array of fur colors. Although we inherit some of our traits from our parents, the environment can also influence them. For example, a tomato plant will turn brown and wilt after a hard frost even if the parent plants prospered, or someone from a long line of runners may end up using a wheelchair if he gets polio. However, these things influenced by the environment will not be passed down to the young.

What Experiences Might Help Children Understand These Ideas?

Sorting the students in the class is an easy way for them to see the variance of traits they have. You can sort by eye color, hairline (widow's peak or straight), dimples or no dimples, or even the appearance of hair on the upper section of the pointer finger. Environmental and inherited traits are easily observed in classmates, and discussing and investigating them can be a valuable way to decide which is which. After the class has taken note of the difference in traits they express, ask them to go further and suppose where those traits came from and why there are so many variances.

> **3-LS4-b.**
> *Construct explanations for how differences in characteristics provide an advantage to some individuals in the same species in surviving, finding mates, and reproducing.*

What Does This Performance Standard Mean?

Animals have many characteristics that help them survive and thrive in the wild. Rabbits that are very white blend in with snow, making them less visible to predators, whereas their browner counterparts are more susceptible to danger. A deer with large antlers will likely be able to protect himself, and a male Lekking fish with bright colors will increase his chances of finding a mate.

What Experiences Might Help Children Understand These Ideas?

Many animals with interesting adaptations and traits can be housed in the classroom and studied. Crayfish are easily kept and provide wonderful examples of traits that aid in protection and in caring for their young. Other, larger animals can be studied simply by looking at pictures of them and thinking critically about why certain traits exist. Why does a giraffe have a long neck, and what would happen if one was born with a shorter one? Why do beavers have such big, sharp teeth, and why don't other rodents have them? Rather than telling the students about these things, encourage them to formulate their own ideas, and ask them to back them up with evidence.

3-LS4-c.
Communicate information about how some characteristics of organisms have been used to inspire the design of technology that meets people's changing needs and wants.

What Does This Performance Standard Mean?

Humans have the amazing ability to make up for the traits we lack by creating things to meet our needs. Since people aren't able to use bioluminescence to see in the dark like the lantern fish, we engineered the lightbulb to increase our productivity during the dark hours of the day. Hippos excrete a pinkish liquid that absorbs UV rays to keep themselves from getting sunburned, but since humans do not have the ability to do this, we created sunscreen. Other animals have many traits that are desirable to humans, and the engineering process allows us to create similar technologies to meet our needs. Whales' use of sonar helped inspire the military to create their own version to locate submarines; likewise, the military uses camouflage patterns to blend into the desert habitat just as the native animals do.

What Experiences Might Help Children Understand These Ideas?

Bio-mimicry or bio-inspiration, the study of how animals' traits can be used to solve human problems, is a relatively new study and is becoming popular with many zoos and animal parks. Many of them have education programs and will bring animals to your school to help students gain knowledge and inspiration from other creatures. Animals can also be studied in books, but instead of simply asking, "What can I learn *about* this animal?" students need to ask, "What can I learn *from* this animal that might help me satisfy a human need or desire?" Students can also study modern technologies that have been inspired by animals and think about where the inspiration came from or how the creator came up with the idea.

3. Self-Investigate

I created a Know, Wonder, Learned chart (see Figure 8.1) during my investigation of this standard to organize my thoughts. Below is my initial chart.

In the first draft of my chart, I went through the standards and thought about how I knew each of them to be true. You will see, however, that at first I didn't have many questions. When I think I understand the

Know	Wonder	Learned
Living things have similar life cycles. Some vocabulary associated with various kinds: *seed, sprout, mature plant, flower, birth, growth, reproduction, death, cocoon,* and *chrysalis.*		
A fruit is actually a part of a plant, but things that we call vegetables are stems, leaves, roots, or flowers.		
Living things often look like their parents, but can also develop traits because of the environment. Everyone says I look like my mom, but she was much tanner than I am because she loved sunbathing so much.	My father is a runner and I also love to run. Is this because I inherited a running gene from my dad or because I watched him run almost every day of my childhood?	
Different versions of traits: hair color and texture, eye color, shape of thumb, size of second toe, etc.		
Children get traits from both parents.	Do you get different traits from each parent (eye color from your mother and thumb shape from your father) or is each trait a mix of both parents?	
Animals that have the right traits to survive in a particular environment will survive longer and will pass on these traits to their children (for example, a giraffe's long neck, a peacock's bright feathers), and change within a species takes a long time.		

Figure 8.1 • My Initial Know, Wonder, Learned Chart

standards completely and don't have many initial questions, I like to go to some outside sources that might prompt more wonderings. A source that I find especially helpful in this process is the radio show *Radiolab*. This show takes the listener through a discussion of scientific and philosophical topics, and although I rarely use it as a source of information, it helps me wonder things I never wondered about before. I listened to an episode on inheritance (www.radiolab.org/2012/nov/19/). Shows covering other topics can be found by using the search tool on the show's website (www.radiolab .org/). After listening to the episode, I added several questions to the "Wonder" column on my chart:

Can environment cause you to develop new traits needed for
   survival?
Can things that happen in a parent's life affect the traits handed
   down to the children?
Can environment change your genetic makeup at all?
Which is more important for survival, good genes or a good
   environment?

Most of these questions were not new to me. Perhaps I had wondered them before, or had a discussion with someone about them at an earlier time. In fact, I might not even end up asking my students to answer these questions, but they are useful because they make me curious, interested, and excited to begin the science unit, and curiosity helps me engage in scientific behaviors. When I am thinking like a scientist, it is easier for me to help my students think like scientists as well.

To investigate the answers to my questions, I chose to watch the video *Genes and Heredity* (Schlessinger 2005). I took notes in the "Learned" column and noted new questions in bold in the "Wonder" column. To answer these new questions, I did an Internet search to find reliable sources that might help me answer them. You will notice that I did not do any investigating about life cycles, since this is a topic that I have already explored in depth and learned about in previous science units.

Each time I found new information, I had new questions that I could have spent days exploring. However, the point is not to know everything. The point is to deepen your content knowledge and begin thinking like a scientist. Following is the final version of my KWL chart (see Figure 8.2):

Know	Wonder	Learned
Living things have similar life cycles. Some vocabulary associated with various kinds: *seed, sprout, mature plant, flower, birth, growth, reproduction, death, cocoon,* and *chrysalis.*		
A fruit is actually a part of a plant, but things that we call vegetables are stems, leaves, roots, or flowers.		
Living things often look like their parents but can also develop traits because of environment. Everyone says I look like my mom, but she was much more tan than I am because she loved sunbathing so much.	My father is a runner and I also love to run. Is this because I inherited a running gene from my dad or because I watched him run almost every day of my childhood?	Gregor Mendel was one of the first scientists to study how genetics works.
Different versions of traits: hair color and texture, eye color, shape of thumb, size of second toe, etc.		Children inherit both dominant and recessive genes. If a gene pair is both dominant (2 tall genes), or both recessive (2 short genes), the child is bred purely for that trait. A mix of both is called hybrid.
Children get traits from both parents.	Do you get different traits from each parent (eye color from your mother and thumb shape from your father) or is each trait a mix of both parents?	Gene combinations can be found using a Punnet (a scientist who studied Mendel's ideas) Square. Purebreds create hybrids that express the dominant trait. Two hybrids have children with a 1 in 4 chance of expressing the recessive trait.
Animals that have the right traits to survive in a particular environment will survive longer and will pass on these traits to their children (for example, a giraffe's long neck, a peacock's bright feathers), and change within a species take a long time.	Can environment cause you to develop new traits needed for survival?	
	Can things that happen in a parent's life affect the traits handed down to the children?	Genes that don't copy exactly create a genetic mutation.
	Can environment change your genetic makeup at all?	Tobacco, UV lights, or chemicals can cause genes to mutate (http://science.howstuffworks.com/life/genetic/dna-mutation.htm). Mutations can be inherited or acquired, and acquired mutations cannot be passed on (http://ghr.nlm.nih.gov/).
	Which is more important for survival, good genes or a good environment?	
	What happens when genes mutate? Can environment cause a mutation?	

Figure 8.2 • My Final Know, Wonder, Learned Chart

4. Plan for Naïve Conceptions

Life cycles are often confusing to children, who think about the entire life span of a plant or animal and have trouble identifying all the stages since they are not isolated events. Similarly, many children have not had enough life experiences to find commonalities between life cycles of different species. Many students still see life as a linear event that begins at birth and ends at death, but are confused about how life starts again.

Students trying to determine where a carrot comes from might say a seed, but when asked where the seed came from, they are often stumped and give answers such as "the grocery store" or "a farmer made it." That a vegetable has a seed somewhere inside it is also a common, naïve conception. This idea makes sense and has merit since many of the things we eat and call vegetables (a cucumber, for example) are really fruits that have visible seeds on the inside. Many fruits (plant parts with seeds inside) are labeled as vegetables by grocery stores, and this can confuse young children. If squash is called a vegetable and has seeds inside, why wouldn't celery also have seeds somewhere in its stalks? Students need to have lots of experiences with many different types of life cycles to confront these naïve conceptions and to be able to formulate ideas that are scientifically accurate.

It is common to believe that an organism can change its genetic material by responding to the environment. Students often believe that giraffes needed to reach the leaves that were high up on the tree, so they continually stretched their necks until they were long enough. They then passed that trait on to their young, and this is why giraffes have long necks. This makes sense, as the traits an animal exhibits often fit the environment in which it lives. This idea is also commonly believed by adults, and is a tough naïve conception to break. Instead of ensuring that students know that environmental traits cannot be passed on, have students focus on the idea that these are traits animals have developed to help them survive in their environment. What if most giraffes had short necks and only a couple were long? Who would survive?

Children's literature can also feed into naïve conceptions about how animals get their traits. Traditional tales are often about how animals changed their traits because of a trick, and explain that that is why the animal still looks that way today. Bear lost his tail in the ice after being tricked by fox, and that is why bears now have short tails. To help students confront these naïve conceptions, involve them in a conversation about them and challenge them to defend their validity or prove the ideas wrong. Encourage them to think about examples in their own lives. If your mother got her ears pierced when she was a child, does that mean that you were born with your ears pierced? Help them make lists of those things that are passed on and those that are not. Students do not need to end up with precise ideas about genetics. Rather, it is more important that they start thinking scientifically.

5. Formulate a Compelling Question

For a question to be compelling to my students, it must be accessible and interesting. Most of the questions I ask go beyond what the standards require and surpass students' current knowledge. My hope is that my question will get them thinking and questioning. I just went to the zoo with my best friend and her two-year-old. My friend was asking me whom I thought the baby looked like: herself or her husband. I thought he looked a little bit like his mom *and* his dad, but I really thought the baby looked like my best friend's grandpa (whom I remember from when I was a child). How is it possible that this new baby looked like a man who has been dead for quite some time?

It is important to note that this question may not cover each of the four disciplinary core ideas. It is only a starting point meant to send the students on an exploration of a topic to get them interested. Follow-up questions may be needed to help the students begin to think about each new idea. It is also possible that the question that you worked so hard on formulating may not work. It may not get the students to talk about what you want them to, or it may not get them thinking enough. That's okay. Do your best with their responses. All it takes is one provocative response and you can get the conversation going. If the conversation really doesn't start, end the session and then go back to the drawing board after the students have left. Think about the results you got and how you can tweak your question to get the results you want. A team is very useful here. Having other minds to help you think through your initial question and to anticipate student responses can create better success in the classroom.

6. Plan for Student Responses

Following is a list of what students might say in response to the opening question:

- People always say I look like my (mom, dad, brother, and so on).
- The way your family looks is the way you will look.

- It's because you get things from your parents. My mom has brown eyes, so I have brown eyes.
- The baby's parents got stuff from the grandfather and the parents gave it to the baby.
- Different traits are passed down from your parents.
- You have genes that decide how you will look.

7. Think Through Responses

Most of the responses I anticipated from the students are somewhat true, blanket statements. It is important that I not confirm them, as that will put a stop to their inquiry. Instead, I use extending talk moves such as "Say more about that" or "What do you mean by that?" Questions will also help the whole class be able to engage. When a student says he has brown eyes because his mom has brown eyes, I might ask, "Does that mean that you always have the same color eyes as your mom? What about your dad?" If students talk about genes, asking them, "What do you mean when you say that word, *genes*?" will help the entire class begin thinking about what the word really means. For the first conversation, I anticipate that the students' responses will be pretty general, and I want to use my responses to help them get more specific.

Remember that after the first lesson is over, repeat Steps 5 through 7 for each new lesson you are going to teach. Use a question from the day before to start with, or share an interesting story that will encourage the students to think about a different content area. As you gain experience with the steps, you'll find that the process takes less and less time. More important, engaging in inquiry to further your content knowledge will help you learn to think like a scientist and help your students do the same.

LEARNING WITH UNDERSTANDING AND TEACHING FOR UNDERSTANDING

Sharon's suggestions for the steps teachers can take to deepen their understanding of science content are the same steps students can take during inquiry to learn about science. Understanding the science you teach is key to being able to teach for understanding. But what does learning with understanding mean?

"Learning for understanding requires not just taking in what you hear; it requires thinking in a number of ways with what you heard—practicing and debugging your thinking until you can make the right connections flexibly" (Perkins 1993, 27).

This type of learning becomes an especially urgent agenda when we think about how children, especially underserved minorities, spend most of their time in school. If our students are memorizing and reciting rather than thinking and doing, they have fewer opportunities to truly understand science concepts.

When we understand something, we can explain it, muster evidence to prove it, make generalizations, find examples and apply the concept in the world, compare it to something similar, and represent the idea in a new way. After her investigation into the life cycles and traits standard, Sharon knew more than just facts. She was able to explain how life cycles are an umbrella concept that connects all living things. She could provide evidence and find examples from real life to explain how we inherit certain traits from our parents. She was able to cite traits that animals have to protect themselves, and explain how these adaptations are analogous to human inventions created for the same purpose. And most important, Sharon was able to take what she learned about life cycles and traits during inquiry and think about how it could be applied to the classroom, so that her students could learn about the concept in meaningful and developmentally appropriate ways. Engaging in the inquiry process deepened Sharon's content knowledge, helping her feel more confident so that rather than teach by telling, she could ask better questions and allow her students to explore and find out for themselves, just as she had.

RESOURCES FOR DEEPENING TEACHERS' SCIENCE CONTENT KNOWLEDGE

Stop Faking It! Finally Understanding Science So You Can Teach It. Series by William C. Robertson, PhD. Published by the National Science Teachers' Association Press, Arlington, VA.

This series provides teachers with easy-to-understand, jargon-free explanations of key science concepts and hands-on activities:

Stop Faking It! Finally Understanding Science So You Can Teach It: Force & Motion
Stop Faking It! Finally Understanding Science So You Can Teach It: Sound
Stop Faking It! Finally Understanding Science So You Can Teach It: Electricity & Magnetism

Stop Faking It! Finally Understanding Science So You Can Teach It: Energy

Stop Faking It! Finally Understanding Science So You Can Teach It: Air, Water, & Weather

Stop Faking It! Finally Understanding Science So You Can Teach It: Chemistry Basics

Stop Faking It! Finally Understanding Science So You Can Teach It: More Chemistry Basics

Uncovering Student Ideas in Science, K–12: Volumes 1, 2, 3, and 4. Series by Page Keeley. Published by the National Science Teachers' Association Press, Arlington, VA.

This series provides teachers with outstanding formative assessment probes and explanations of key concepts in all areas of science.

A Private Universe Project: Teachers' Lab, by the Annenberg/CPB Math and Science Project

This website provides teachers with information and in-class activities that further content knowledge about the phases of the moon and the reasons for the seasons: www.learner.org/teacherslab/pup/index.html.

Lunar Phase Simulator

This website shows a visual demonstration of the phases of the moon: http://astro.unl.edu/naap/lps/animations/lps.html.

Fossil Finders

This website from Cornell University provides teachers with science content, curriculum projects, and professional development opportunities that focus on paleontology: www.fossilfinders.org.

Annenberg Learner

This website is devoted to the professional development of K–12 teachers. The site provides videos, explanations, and interactive activities for many science topics. In addition, it discusses common misconceptions and allows you to take a quiz to see where your knowledge level lies: http://learner.org.

Schlessinger Media

This video series provides hundreds of videos about many science topics. Titles can be purchased on their website or viewed in Safari Montage: www.libraryvideo.com.

REFERENCES

Abruscato, Jack. 2004. *Teaching Children Science: A Discovery Approach*. New York: Pearson.

Alonzo, A. C. 2002. "Evaluation of a Model for Supporting the Development of Elementary School Teachers' Science Content Knowledge." *Proceedings of the Annual International Conference of the Association for the Education of Teachers in Science*. Charlotte, NC.

Brady, Kathryn, Mary Beth Forton, and Deborah Porter. 2011. *Rules in School: Teaching Discipline in the Responsive Classroom*. Greenfield, MA: Northeast Foundation for Children.

Bransford, John D., Ann L. Brown, and Rodney R. Cocking. 2000. *How People Learn: Brain, Mind, Experience, and School*. Washington, DC: National Academies Press.

Bresser, Rusty, Kathy Melanese, and Christine Sphar. 2009. *Supporting English Language Learners in Math Class*. Sausalito, CA: Math Solutions.

Broderick, Alicia, Heeral Mehta-Parekh, and D. Kim Reid. 2005. "Differentiating Instruction for Disabled Students in Inclusive Classrooms." *Theory into Practice* 44 (3): 194–202.

California Commission on Teacher Credentialing. 2008. *CalTPA Handbook*. Sacramento: California Commission on Teacher Credentialing.

Carr, John, Ursula Sexton, and Rachel Lagunoff. 2007. *Making Science Accessible to English Learners: A Guidebook for Teachers*. San Francisco: Center for Teaching and Learning at WestEd.

Chapin, Suzanne H., Catherine O'Connor, and Nancy C. Anderson. 2011. *Classroom Discussions: Seeing Math Discourse in Action*. Sausalito, CA: Math Solutions.

Charney, Ruth. 2002. *Teaching Children to Care: Classroom Management for Ethical and Academic Growth*. Greenfield, MA: Northeast Foundation for Children.

Cloud, Nancy, Fred Genesee, and Else Hamayan. 2009. *Literacy Instruction for English Language Learners: A Teacher's Guide to Research-Based Practices*. Portsmouth, NH: Heinemann.

Committee on Conceptual Framework for the New K–12 Science Education Standards. 2012. *A Framework for K–12 Science Education: Practices, Crosscutting Concepts, and Core Ideas*. Washington, DC: National Academies Press.

Cuevas, Peggy, Okhee Lee, Juliet Hart, and Rachael Deaktor. 2005. "Improving Science Inquiry with Elementary Students of Diverse Backgrounds." *Journal of Research in Science Teaching* 42 (3): 337–357.

Delpit, Lisa. 1999. *Other People's Children: Cultural Conflict in the Classroom*. New York: The New Press.

———. 2012. *Multiplication Is for White People: Raising Expectations for Other People's Children*. New York: The New Press.

Dorf, Rena, Patrick M. Shields, Juliet Tiffany-Morales, Ardice Hartry, Teresa McCaffrey, John McDonald, Holly Jacobson, Margaret Gaston, Patsy Wilkes, and Linda Bond. 2011. *High Hopes: The State of Science Education in California*. San Francisco: Center for Teaching and Learning at WestEd.

Einstein, Albert. 1936. "Physics and Reality." *Journal of the Franklin Institute* 221 (3): 349–382.

Friere, Paolo. 1970. *Pedagogy of the Oppressed*. New York: The Seabury Press.

Geier, Robert, Phyllis C. Blumenfeld, Ronald W. Marx, Joseph S. Krajcik, Barry Fishman, Elliot Soloway, and Juanita Clay-Chambers. 2008. "Standardized Test Outcomes for Students Engaged in Inquiry-Based Science Curricula in the Context of Urban Reform." *Journal of Research in Science Teaching* 45 (8): 922–939.

Haberman, Martin. 1991. "The Pedagogy of Poverty Versus Good Teaching." *Phi Delta Kappan* 74 (4): 290–294.

Hammer, David, Fred Goldberg, and Sharon Fargason. 2012. "Responsive Teaching and the Beginnings of Energy in a Third-Grade Classroom." *Review of Science, Mathematics, and ICT Education* 6 (1): 51–72.

Hill, Jane, and Kathleen M. Flynn. 2006. *Classroom Instruction That Works with English Language Learners*. Alexandria, VA: Association of Supervision and Curriculum Development.

Houk, Farin. 2005. *Supporting English Language Learners: A Guide for Teachers and Administrators*. Portsmouth, NH: Heinemann.

Kohn, Alfie. 2011. "Poor Teaching for Poor Children? In the Name of School Reform." *Education Week* 30 (20): 32–33.

Kriete, Roxann. 2002. *The Morning Meeting Book.* Greenfield, MA: Northeast Foundation for Children.

Lawrence Hall of Science. 2012. Full Option Science System (FOSS). Berkeley, CA: The Lawrence Hall of Science. http://lhsfoss.org.

Moll, Luis C., Cathy Amanti, Deborah Neff, and Norma Gonzalez. 1992. "Funds of Knowledge for Teaching: Using a Qualitative Approach to Connect Homes and Classrooms." *Theory into Practice* 31 (2): 132–141.

National Committee on Science Education Standards and National Research Council. 1996. *National Science Education Standards.* Washington, DC: National Academies Press.

National Research Council. 2012. *A Framework for K–12 Science Education: Practices, Crosscutting Concepts, and Core Ideas.* Washington, DC: National Academies Press.

Next Generation Science Standards Writing Team. 2012. *Next Generation Science Standards.* Washington, DC: National Academies Press. www.nextgenscience.org.

Ohanian, Susan. 1999. *One Size Fits Few: The Folly of Educational Standards.* Portsmouth, NH: Heinemann.

Ornstein, Avi. 2006. "The Frequency of Hands-on Experimentation and Student Attitudes Towards Science: A Statistically Significant Relation." *Journal of Science Education and Technology* 15 (3): 285–296.

Pearce, Charles R. 1999. *Nurturing Inquiry: Real Science for the Elementary Classroom.* Portsmouth, NH: Heinemann.

Perkins, David. 1993. "Teaching for Understanding." *American Educator* 17 (3): 27–35.

Rogers, Virginia M. 1972. "Innovation Through Experimentation." *Educational Leadership* 29 (4): 301.

Rosebery, Ann S., Beth Warren, and Faith R. Conant. 1992. "Appropriating Scientific Discourse: Findings from Language Minority Classrooms." *Journal of Research in Science Teaching* 33: 569–600.

Saul, Wendy, and Jeanne Reardon. 1996. *Beyond the Science Kit: Inquiry in Action.* Portsmouth, NH: Heinemann.

Schlessinger Media. 2000. *All About the Transfer of Energy.* Wynnewood, PA: Schlessinger Media.

———. 2005. *Genes and Heredity.* Wynnewood, PA: Schlessinger Media.

Science Advisory Blue Ribbon Panel. 2009. Final Report: Assessment of Science Education and Recommendations for Improving Science Performance in SDUSD. San Diego [CA] Unified School District.

Shulman, Lee S. 1986. "Those Who Understand: Knowledge Growth in Teaching." *Educational Researcher* 15 (2): 4–14.

Trundle, Kathy Cabe, Ronald Atwood, and John E. Christopher. 2006. "Preservice Elementary Teachers' Knowledge of Observable Moon Phases and Pattern of Change in Phases." *Journal of Science Teacher Education* 17: 87–101.

Wagner, Tony. 2008. *The Global Achievement Gap: Why Even Our Best Schools Don't Teach the Survival Skills Our Children Need and What We Can Do About It.* New York: Basic Books.

Watson, Bruce, and Richard Konicek. 1990. "Teaching for Conceptual Change: Confronting Children's Experience." *Phi Delta Kappan* 71 (9): 680–685.

Wilson, Christopher D., Joseph A. Taylor, Susan M. Kowalski, and Janet Carlson. 2010. "The Relative Effects and Equity of Inquiry-Based and Commonplace Science Teaching on Students' Knowledge, Reasoning, and Argumentation." *Journal of Research in Science Teaching* 47 (3): 276–301.

Woodford, Chris. 2000/2009. *Batteries.* Available online at www.explainthatstuff.com/batteries.html.

Wright, Wayne E. 2010. *Foundations for Teaching English Language Learners: Research, Theory, Policy, and Practice.* Philadelphia: Caslon.

Yin, Yue, Miki K. Tomita, and Richard J. Shavelson. 2008. "Diagnosing and Dealing with Student Misconceptions: Floating and Sinking." *Science Scope* 31 (8): 34–39.

Zemelman, Steven, Harvey Daniels, and Arthur Hyde. 2005. *Best Practice: New Standards for Teaching and Learning in America's Schools.* 3rd ed. Portsmouth, NH: Heinemann.

INDEX

Page numbers followed by an *f* indicate figures.

engagement, 95–97, 95*f*, 96*f*, 97*f*
English language learners. *See also* diverse classrooms
    académic language and, 63–64
    access to content, 74
    challenges faced by, 62–63
    content and language objectives, 64–66
    energy unit, 96, 108, 112–113, 120
    group work, 55
    morning meeting and, 46
    overview, 61–62
    supporting, 10–11, 66–74, 67*f*, 69*f*, 71*f*–72*f*, 74*f*
    UV bead unit, 82–83
expectations, 55–56, 75–76
experience, 3–5
experimentation
    energy unit, 107–110, 108*f*, 109*f*
    UV bead unit, 84–87, 86*f*
explaining
    of answers given during inquiry science, 142–144
    English language learners and, 72*f*
exploration, 95–97, 95*f*, 96*f*, 97*f*

F
familiarity, 41
family, communication with, 84
FOSS: Full Option Science System, 3
Friere, Paolo, 151
funds of knowledge, 83

G
generalization, 4–5
global achievement gap, 130
Global Achievement Gap, The (Wagner), 130
Gribble, David, 9
group work. *See also* small-group discussions
    classroom management and, 54–56, 55*f*
    energy unit, 98–99, 104–106, 104*f*
    English language learners, 67–68, 67*f*
    students changing their minds, 136–138
    UV bead unit, 88–89
    when students already know the answers, 140–142, 141*f*
guiding principles. *See also* inquiry science
    assessment, 28–30
    background of students, 18–20, 25–28
    communication with students, 31–37, 32*f*, 33*f*
    curriculum, 30–31
    designing effective learning environments, 37
    disequilibrium, 24–25
    having all the answers, 16–18
    ideas that may or may not be scientifically accurate, 23–24
    models, 22–23, 23*f*
    overview, 16
    science as a team effort, 20–21, 21*f*
    scientific knowledge of students, 18–20

H
Haberman, Martin, 93
hands-on science, 2–3, 7–9, 15–16
having all the answers, 16–18
Hehta-Parekh, Heeral, 144
high-stakes testing. *See* testing
home-school connection, 83–84
How People Learn (Bransford, Brown, and Cocking), 37
Hyde, Arthur, 17
hypothesizing. *See also* questioning; testable questions
    energy unit, 109–110, 109*f*, 114–116, 121–122
    English language learners and, 72*f*
    students changing their minds and, 136–138
    UV bead unit, 80–81

I
ideas that may or may not be scientifically accurate, 23–24
identifying, 72*f*
ignoring type of response, 32*f*. *See also* communication with students
independence, classroom management and, 57–58
individualized education plan (IEP) goals, 144–146
inheritance, Next Generation Science Standards and, 159–168, 163*f*, 165*f*
inquiry overview, 1–5
inquiry science. *See also* guiding principles
    academic language, 63–64
    classroom management, 39–40
    compared to hands-on science, 7–9
    curriculum, 131–132
    English language learners, 62–64
    example of, 5–7
    getting stuck, 139–140
    naïve conceptions, 3–5
    overview, 1–3, 15–16, 129–131
    scientific facts, 149–151, 150*f*
    students changing their minds, 136–138, 138*f*
interruptions, 43–44
investigation
    energy unit, 107–109, 108*f*
    naïve conceptions, 4–5
    teacher's content knowledge and, 155–157

J
journaling. *See* science journals; writing

K
kindness, 41
Know, Wonder, Learned (KWL) chart
    Next Generation Science Standards, 163–164, 163*f*, 165*f*
    teacher's content knowledge, 156